Live Your Calling

A 40-Day Devotional for Women Leaders

womenleaders.com

Live Your Calling
A 40-Day Devotional for Women Leaders

From WomenLeaders.com

Copyright © 2016 | Christianity Today

Published by Christianity Today,
465 Gundersen Dr., Carol Stream, IL 60188

Printed in the U.S.A.

WomenLeaders.com | ChristianityToday.org

WOMENLEADERS.COM TEAM
PUBLISHER: Kevin A. Miller
EDITOR: Amy Jackson
DESIGN: Jillian Hathaway
MARKETING: Kristen Cloyd

womenleaders.com

Live Your Calling
A 40-Day Devotional for Women Leaders

Though the Bible was written in a time and culture that saw women as basically worthless, voiceless, and untrustworthy, God's Word says something very different about women.

Miriam led Israel in worship. Deborah called and accompanied a reluctant Barak into battle. Huldah boldly served as a prophet for King Josiah. Esther courageously used her influence to save the Jewish people. Ruth saved Jesus' lineage by showing incredible faith and working alongside Boaz.

The Samaritan woman at the well became the first person to bring the good news to the Gentiles. Mary and Martha were dear friends of Jesus, and Jesus even held up Mary as an example. Women were the first to discover the empty tomb, and Mary Magdalene was the first person to proclaim the good news of the Resurrection. Lydia and Nympha hosted house churches in the early days of Christianity. And Priscilla partnered with her husband to correct Apollos' teaching.

When I read the Bible, it's clear that God has important work for women to do. Yet even when we know we're called by God, it can be difficult to fully live that calling. Women unfortunately face a lot of obstacles and barriers—both internal and external—that can keep us from obeying God's call on our lives. But I believe God's "yes" needs to overcome every "no" we hear from ourselves and the world.

At WomenLeaders.com, we believe you have an important role to play in God's kingdom work. We're for you, and we value what you uniquely bring to the table. What's more: we're convinced we need you—your voice, gifts, perspectives, and leadership. So this devotional is designed just for you. The 40 devotions are written by women leaders to women leaders, and include diverse voices and experiences.

Over eight weeks, you'll be encouraged to gain clarity in your calling, focus on your identity in Christ, get the rest and care you need to be a healthy leader, lead authentically and vulnerably, face difficult days with confidence, and take bold steps to fully live your calling. My prayer is that you will be empowered to live your calling in audacious new ways, fully surrendered to God.

AMY JACKSON
Managing Editor of WomenLeaders.com

How To Use This Devotional

This devotional is perfect for your own individual reflection. There are 8 weeks of devotional content, with 5 devotions each week, which include Scripture passages and reflection questions. Each week also includes suggested weekend activities for going deeper into the week's topic, such as journaling exercises, further Bible study, and specific action steps.

You can also use this devotional in a group setting. To help you facilitate your time together, each week includes group ideas that incorporate questions and activities you can do as a group. This resource would work especially well with a group of fellow women leaders—whether from your own church or a variety of churches in your community. If you're considering forming a support group, this is the perfect resource to use as you get started.

Join the Conversation

We'd love to hear how *Live Your Calling* is impacting your life. Share pictures of your group, stories about your calling, and more.

Hashtags	#WomenLeadersDevotional #LiveYourCalling
Facebook	WomenLeadersCom
Twitter	@WomenLeadersCom
Website	WomenLeaders.com

Table of Contents

Week 1

You Are Needed

Empowered Women Leaders

Psalm 139:13–16

What does it really mean to be empowered? With so much chatter over the years about "girl power," it's easy to dismiss the notion of empowering women as a mere cheer from the stands—"Rah rah, go girls!"—or an agenda that seeks to promote girls over boys. But it's so much more than that.

The fact that we strive to empower women may suggest that women in some way are not powerful, but that isn't true. Women are powerful in profound ways. I saw this most clearly when I went to Africa and met women in Kenya who were determined to bring clean water to their village. They worked on a plan for 10 years before they actually began to see the fruits of their labor. Now that water flows freely in their community, these women dream about finding ways to bring water to their friends and family in neighboring villages.

Closer to home, I see empowered women every day at work, in my community, at my church, and in my family. I see an empowered woman in my neighbor, the single mom who reinvented her life after her husband walked out and left her to raise a daughter on her own. I see an empowered woman in the widow down the block who found her way back to joy after many years of grieving her husband's passing. I see an empowered woman in my 50-something sister who decided to return to school to finish her bachelor's degree and go on for her master's so she could change careers. Wherever women are discovering and utilizing their unique gifts and courageously living the life God has called them to live, even when faced with challenging life circumstances, these are empowered women.

We all know them when we see them.

The world never benefits when we shrink back, play small, or give up using our gifts. Whether you're a full-time ministry leader, a school teacher, a stay-at-home mom, or a high-powered professional, each of us has a particular journey.

We also need to look at how God's intention for women originated with his creation of Eve. Contrary to what we often think, when God created a "suitable helper" for Adam in Eve, she became the embodiment of what it means to be an empowered woman. She was made to be his partner in God's mission. We quickly learn that even strong women are susceptible to sin, but Eve, in her original design, was God's perfect plan for women. As strong women, we need to revisit Eve in the garden and reclaim the image of God

we share with her. As we do, we'll find that empowered women are exactly what the world needs.

MARIAN V. LIAUTAUD is director of marketing at Aspen Group.

Reflect

When are you tempted to shrink back, play small, or give up using your gifts?

The Flawed Women of History

1 Corinthians 1:26–31

have a long history with Wonder Woman, mostly involving the '70s TV show starring beauty queen Lynda Carter. An Amazonian superhero, Wonder Woman wore magic silver bracelets that repelled bullets, flew an invisible airplane, and wore a golden lasso on her hip that could trap and hold any villain. Episode after episode, Wonder Woman vanquished her enemies with strength and smarts, yet somehow her lipstick stayed a perfect glossy red and her shiny brunette hair never went flat. On top of this, Wonder Woman maintained a no-kill policy and was genuinely nice.

As I grew older, I kept an eye out for other strong women. Oh, there were women like Betsy Ross and Pocahontas, whom I learned about from history class, but stitching together a flag or bringing food to the English settlers didn't quench my thirst for a female hero—until I learned about Rosie the Riveter.

Getting to know Rosie whetted my appetite to find more women who, with grit and guts, changed the world like Mother Teresa, Harriet Tubman, Eleanor Roosevelt, Jane Austen, Mary Magdalene, and Perpetua. But as I encountered these women of history, I felt a familiar sense of inadequacy; their strength, intelligence, power, and breadth of talent seemed far beyond mine.

But the more I got to know them, the more I realized these women were just like me. Real, flawed, broken. They often lacked education, resources, and support, and they had to overcome ignorance, tradition, prejudice, and fear. They also faced significant obstacles. Escaped slave Harriet Tubman, who led 300 people to safety on the Underground Railroad, suffered horrific abuse along with a traumatic brain injury that almost killed her as a teen. Elizabeth Fry, who reformed the entire prison system in England, struggled with debilitating periods of mental illness. Eleanor Roosevelt, a great humanitarian, was buffeted by virulent criticism of her less than glamorous appearance and wrecked by her husband's infidelity, yet she became FDR's active political partner in a presidency that successfully led the United States out of a devastating world war and paralyzing economic depression.

Forget Wonder Woman. You don't need magic bracelets or a golden lasso to change the world. You don't have to be Harriet Tubman or Eleanor Roosevelt, either. To make a difference, just look around and say: "What can I do that isn't going to get done unless I do it, just because of who I am?"

You, too, can become a woman who changes the world by starting in your own backyard. And if God wants it to turn into something larger, that's up to him. If you do what you can, with the tools and resources God has given you, then who knows what can happen?

SUSY FLORY is a *New York Times* bestselling author, speaker, writer's conference director, and collaborative writer.

Reflect
When are you tempted to believe you are inadequate to impact the world?

Missing: Women Leaders

Joel 2:28-32

sat in the front row listening intently to a woman who taught from the Bible with wisdom, grace, and knowledge. She mesmerized me. Like a sponge, I soaked up every bit of wisdom she poured forth. The impact she had on me and hundreds of other women that day was immeasurable as she encouraged us to be more fully devoted to Christ.

This amazing teacher wasn't on staff at the church, though. In fact, there were no women on staff or in any leadership roles. Other than "pastor's wife," she had no official role or title. This didn't surprise me. At the time, I didn't know any women who were paid pastors or church leaders. I had no model for what women in ministry could look like, and that was troubling to me.

Since I was a little girl, I've felt a stirring in my heart to serve in the local church. I felt called to ministry, yet I didn't see any way to fulfill that call. So I ignored it for years. When I started attending another church where women in leadership were valued, however, everything changed. The woman in charge of small groups saw leadership potential in me and encouraged me to lead a group. Ten years later, I'm a pastor and a small-group director. Now I have the great joy and opportunity to help other people move into leadership roles.

Sadly, women leaders are not well represented in our churches. Without women leaders only part of God's image is reflected. Before the fall, men and women related to each other as co-rulers, both made in the image of God, taking dominion of the earth together. As a result of the fall, this beautiful synergy between Adam and Eve was tragically skewed. God's redemptive plan is to restore everything destroyed by sin, including male-female relationships.

The church—and the world—need what women leaders uniquely offer. We are nurturers, team builders, collaborators, prayer warriors, and strategists. We bring compassion, tenderness, transparency, vulnerability, encouragement, and wisdom. Without women leaders in the church, only half of what the church has to offer is expressed.

Recently, I noticed a cluster of women gathering around a small-group leader named Kara in our church lobby. The people around her were silent, hanging on every word. Watching Kara that Sunday morning made me smile, remembering when I first recognized her leadership potential. Over the years, we've only seen Kara grow in her leadership. We've intentionally invested in her and guided her toward her next steps in leadership. But the first step was simply recognizing her potential. Sadly, seeing the potential in women leaders isn't happening in all churches. But more women leaders are desperately needed—including you.

JULIA MATEER is a writer, speaker, therapist, and director of women's small groups at Bayside Community Church, a multi-campus church in Florida.

Reflect

What do you think the church misses out on when women leaders are sidelined?

Bossy Little Girls

Proverbs 1:20-27

When I became pregnant, I often wondered whether the baby was a boy or girl. As I thought about my future with a daughter, there was one fear that weighed heavily on my heart: As a mother, how could I prevent my daughter from becoming a bossy little girl?

To be honest, I was that bossy little girl when I was young, and I was nervous that I wouldn't be able to help my potential daughter navigate her strengths and leadership in a more helpful manner. When I was growing up, adults were very intentional about teaching boys to harness their strength. This emphasis manifested itself in many different ways, but it was especially apparent in the commandment that under no circumstances should a boy ever, ever hit a girl.

I am grateful that adults took the time to convey this message to boys—it's an important one. But the funny thing is that adults spent less time teaching girls how to harness their strength. Perhaps this is because girls are, in general, smaller and less physically threatening, but that is not the only way to measure strength. Girls and women are very strong, and one of the ways females exercise their strength is through verbal communication—the abuse of which is sometimes bossiness.

The Bible provides us with countless examples of both the good uses and horrible abuses of female strength: Rebekah cunningly manipulated her sons and deceived her husband to acquire Jacob's blessing; Esther courageously used her influence to save the Jewish people; Delilah exploited her marriage to bring about the downfall of Samson and his people; and Joanna, manager of Herod's household, financially supported Jesus and the disciples.

Although journalists like Nicholas Kristof and Sheryl WuDunn, authors of *Half the Sky: Turning Oppression Into Opportunity for Women Worldwide*, have shed light on the powerlessness of many women throughout the world, it is also worth remembering that woman are inherently strong. God has granted us unique strengths that we can use either to build up God's kingdom or to selfishly rebel.

Whether or not my hypothesis about little girls is true, women undoubtedly have strengths that need to be cultivated correctly. The more common conversation among women in the church concerns hardship and overcoming struggle, but that narrative needs to be supplemented. In addition to helping women overcome, the church should also help women identify their gifts and their strengths.

If we fail to do this, the strengths of Christian women are not only likely to go unused, but might even be misused.

SHARON HODDE MILLER is a writer, speaker, pastor's wife, and mom. She earned her PhD on the subject of women and calling.

Reflect
How were you taught to harness your strengths and leadership gifts?

Leading from "Deficits"

2 Corinthians 12:9-10

Growing up, I was a child at risk. We had close to nothing, including Christmases without gifts, times when the refrigerator was empty, and winter days without heat. As a poor Hispanic-Latina family, we had no wealthy relatives or networks to rely on. Our difficult circumstances drove me to God, though. He was all I had, so I clung to him.

I grew up with lots of deficits in my life: poverty, mental illness in my family, and a minority status. And once I began attending a Christian college I learned I had one more: my sex. This new revelation disoriented me. For years, I'd wanted to attend seminary, but now I thought it was off-limits. My husband encouraged me to go anyway, and it turned out to be one of the best decisions of my life. There, my gifts were encouraged, and I was told to consider becoming a theology professor.

After seminary, I hosted and produced a live radio program where I taught from the Bible and played music. I had a diverse cross-section of listeners from

20

different ethnic backgrounds and denominations. Later, when my husband and I moved, I was invited to be one of five teaching leaders at an urban church plant, and I gave messages once or twice a month. I was the only woman on the team, and not everyone at the church believed women were allowed to give sermons. But they admitted that I was invited by the four male leaders and that I did have a gift, which in the end was very affirming.

While I once viewed my past as a liability, I now view it as a strength. As a result of the "deficits" I've experienced, I have compassion for the poor, the disadvantaged, the marginalized, and those who feel invisible. I'm not afraid to lovingly speak up when I see something wrong, and I can easily talk and write about theology.

Churches need the perspective that comes from women in leadership—people who have experienced deficits in life. I've seen precarious situations nearly bungled because some of my dear brothers simply did not have a woman's insight or experience. I often find myself wincing when I consider the many situations that are mishandled and the lives that are damaged because many women have no say and no leadership roles in their churches.

In a fantastic turn of events, God has given me the opportunity to publish a book on spiritual formation and teach in a seminary where I am helping to form the spiritual lives of my brothers and sisters who are pastors, aspiring pastors, or lay leaders. In addition, I serve as Minister of Pastoral Care at my church. Like Paul, I see how through my perceived weaknesses and disadvantages God has made me stronger, more compassionate, and more justice-oriented. And that makes me a better leader.

MARLENA GRAVES is a writer, speaker, and the author of *A Beautiful Disaster.*

Reflect
What "deficits" in your life has God turned into gifts for ministry?

Weekend Ideas

1. Take time to learn about a few women leaders from history. You can choose someone mentioned in "The Flawed Women of History" or someone you've always wanted to know more about. If you need suggestions of where to start, try Catherine Booth or Sojourner Truth. How did God use them for his kingdom?

2. Women bring something unique to the world and to the church. To find some inspiration, watch a movie about the power of women. For a few suggestions, try *Half the Sky, Erin Brockovich, The Secret Life of Bees, The Help*, or *A League of Their Own*.

3. Journal about the things you were taught growing up about being a girl. Were you taught to be quiet? Polite? Were you told there were things you couldn't or shouldn't do? How do these early messages about gender affect you today?

4. Read 2 Corinthians 12:9–10 again. Journal about the weaknesses or "deficits" that you have allowed to hold you back. Then turn them over to God. What does he say about these weaknesses?

5. Read Ephesians 2:1–10 again. Notice especially verse 10. What does it mean that you are God's handiwork? Do you believe this? Do you act like it?

Group Ideas

1. If your group members decided to learn more about a woman from history or watch a movie about women, share what you learned with the group. How are you impacted by what you learned?

2. If your group members journaled about what they were taught growing up about being a girl, share those insights with each other. How were you empowered by those early messages? How were you held back? What do you want to tell young girls instead?

3. Use "The Flawed Women of History" as the basis for your discussion. Read the Scripture passage together. Then discuss: What women leaders do you look to for inspiration? What did they do to impact the world? When are you tempted to believe you are inadequate to impact the world? What excuses have you used to hold you back from what God is calling you to?

Week 2

Clear Calling

Out of the Box

2 Timothy 1:6–12

One pastor, when asked about his calling, said, "God owns me. Period. I am completely and totally his. When you are called, you will do extraordinary things because you are always obedient to God. God uses the obedient Christian."

I've felt that calling. Focused on a specific spiritual issue, my eyes twinkle, my voice raises a notch, and I feel as if every cell in my body has just been elevated to alert status. My mind kicks in with reasoning powers that aren't available for other issues. When I'm consumed by my calling, for a split second a spotlight hits and I recognize its heavenly origin. I am both exhilarated and humbled. I rejoice in every second of enlightenment. All too soon the moment is over. The article, conversation, or teaching session is put aside. The spotlight dims and I put the "calling" back in the box, as if this gift from God were only a loan.

But what if I didn't put it back in the box? What if God meant for each of us to make it permanent? What if he expected us to live our calling 24/7? Should it become a permanent part of us until it changes who we are? What if it became the burning bush that engulfed our every thought, wish, relationship, and deed? If our calling never left us, perhaps we would be better mothers, wives, friends, and ambassadors for Christ.

Some leaders neglect their families in order to give everything to God. We rightly encourage them to be more "present" or aware of daily relationships. That causes some to compartmentalize their work. Like me, their calling goes back in the box. God did not intend for our calling to disappear when we clock out of spiritual work.

The heavenly answer is not to put our calling aside but to allow it to define who we are. When the called are consumed with the calling, we are better people, more rested, and even friendlier. When our calling is more like the life of Jesus, our personal life can only follow suit. Not once did Jesus ever change. He was Jesus every moment of every day. When he rested, he was the Son of God. When he preached, he was the Son of God. When he had pity on the poor, he was the Son of God. When he attended a wedding, he was the Son of God.

When you are called, you will reflect Christ every moment of every day, and his power will allow you to draw on that call for strength, passion, and endurance to do his will.

DEBBIE JANSEN is a family specialist, author, speaker, minister, and counselor.

Reflect
Do you see your calling as something that only comes out at certain times, or something that affects all of your life?

Who Are You?

Psalm 139:1–10

Purpose and calling are not as mysterious as we sometimes believe they are. They are with us from the beginning of our lives, and they unfold as we grow and change. Your purpose is not specific to your professional work or any of the other roles you play. You were created with intentionality that transcends your circumstances. You were not put here simply to do anything—you were put here to be you. And you are a specialist at doing just that. In fact, you're the only one with the necessary qualifications. While you may be called to different roles or relationships at various points in your life, ultimately, your calling is not something to do. It is someone to be. It is rooted in the person you are at your core. And here's even better news: You don't really have to find it. It's already with you.

Now, even though you have been you since the day you were born, you may not be entirely sure who that person is. After all, our true selves can be easily buried under a mountain of expectations, a cloak of shame, and a deluge of self-protection, second guessing, and crushing self-doubt. You may have spent

28

nearly every day of your life trying to be someone else. You may be so good at it, you actually think that person you're trying to be really is you. You may be tremendously out of touch with your true self, and you may need some help to find her.

You can find clues to who you are by looking back to moments in your life when you have felt fully alive. Consider a few times when you have felt your full power as a human being made in the image of God. Your body and mind were in the same brilliant zone, working together seamlessly. You weren't thinking about what other people thought of you. Almost electrified, you were so engrossed in what you were doing that time nearly stopped.

Maybe you were running through the grass on your front lawn. Exploring the creek on Grandma's farm. Painting what your imagination saw, building a model airplane, writing a poem, listening to music or making it, hosting a party, helping a friend, swimming laps, preaching a sermon. Maybe you were all alone, or surrounded by people. Perhaps you were full of joy, or your heart was at peace, or you felt a deep connection to God. Whatever the circumstances, whatever the time in your life, that zone tells you something about you. It points to the person you were made to be.

That person is you. Do you know her?

Rather than get caught up in figuring out what you should do, I encourage you to get back in touch with your true self, then to ask yourself how you can best be the person you have discovered in those "in the zone" moments. That's what you're here for.

AMY SIMPSON is an inner strength coach, a popular speaker, and the award-winning author of *Troubled Minds: Mental Illness and the Church's Mission* and *Anxious: Choosing Faith in a World of Worry.*

Reflect

Think about a time you felt fully alive, even electrified. What were you doing? With whom?

Proactive Listening

Philippians 1:3–11

was 19 when I met Amy Orr-Ewing, the British speaker, writer, and evangelist. We were both students at Oxford University at the time, and we met through the student ministry at St. Aldates Church—a lively group that went by the memorable, slightly awkward name of "Risky Living." But Amy and her now-husband, Frog, did, in fact, embody some of the riskiest living I'd ever seen in Christian peers, and that's still the case today.

Currently, Amy writes books, teaches, and trains in evangelism, and co-leads a unique and growing church. While she wears many hats, she is anchored by a central calling to evangelism and apologetics. Amy is an inspiring example of a woman passionately and relentlessly pursuing her calling, and encouraging others to do the same.

"In moving into my calling, there was a combination of being proactive—pushing on doors and exploring options—and also asking God to guide me through his Word, my dreams and passions, the prophetic, and the circumstances I found myself in," Orr-Ewing says. She sees more anxiety about vocation today than when she was a young adult. "In my era, we prayed it through, and then started off; we felt that God could guide us supernaturally during the process. But today it seems harder, and I see more hesitation and concern along the lines of 'I'm not sure;' 'Is this right?' 'Am I hearing God?' I try to encourage young leaders to try things—to go for it. God can speak to us as we go."

Orr-Ewing fields plenty of questions from her audiences, especially about how to identify one's calling. The first things to consider are the gifts, training, and opportunities God uniquely gives to each person. Then, she refers to the dreams and passions of the heart, those activities or communities one's drawn to. Lastly, she unpacks what she and her husband call the three P's. "The first P is people—who are the people God's put in my life to serve with, to journey with in my work? The second P is purpose—hearing from God what he wants us to do through the Bible, prophetic words God gives us, or words from other people. And the third P is place—where has God put you? Start where you are. Even for those of us who are called to work internationally, we are still to have a rootedness and involvement in our home locale."

While Amy has a well-defined and prominent career, she's no stranger to the average Christian's modern-world struggle to nail down calling. The abundant opportunities in our hyperconnected world can heap doubt and insecurity onto even the most intentional. The Christian version of "FOMO" (fear of missing out) can be a fear that our efforts to serve God are too small or insufficient. She emphasizes that smaller in scale, however, is not smaller in importance. She knows the Sunday school class she teaches for 10-year-old boys at her church is just as important, kingdom-wise, as a talk she may give to staffers on Capitol Hill. "I passionately believe the two are just as significant in God's eyes."

SUSAN ARICO is a consultant, providing strategic and program-related assistance to Christian nonprofits.

Reflect

How has God revealed your calling to you? Was it in an expected way, or more of a surprise?

What You Can't Not Do

Exodus 15:19–21

If I could just get this next job ... If I just had enough money for a babysitter ... If I could just finish my degree ... If my church would just hire me. How many of us have suffered under the tyranny of the "just?" *Just* is a word we should remove from our vocabulary.

The word "calling" is defined as "a strong urge toward a particular way of life or career." Calling goes far beyond anything we find on the other side of "just." And because of that, the path to our calling is never "just" around the next corner. Rather, calling is about becoming a lifelong explorer, and refusing to believe that we are defined by one job, one relationship, or one season of life. Because of that, finding the shape of our call takes time, work, trial, and error.

You have a calling. God is actively, certainly calling you to something. He calls in many ways. He called Moses with a burning bush. He called Miriam through her family and her gifts for song and speech. He called Hannah through the waiting, and he called Mary through an angel. He called Paul through a blinding light and Nicodemus through a conversation in the dark. He is not limited in his creativity and he's not nervous about your timeline. He's looking for humble hearts that are fully devoted to him and willing to do anything to move his kingdom forward. He equips us for the work he wants us to do, not the work we think we want to do. And he uses all of our lives—our waiting places, our frustrations, our experiences, and our gifts—to shape us into women who will be strong enough for the call he will place on our lives.

In my own season of wrestling with calling, I had the opportunity to hear author Parker Palmer speak. His words were helpful: "Your calling is anything that you can't not do." When we're young, sometimes we think there are a million things "we can't not do." But with experience, with waiting, with humbling ourselves and allowing God to shape us into souls he can use, our calling becomes clearer. We begin to make decisions based on the broad strokes of things "we can't not do"—like showing mercy, working for justice, or embracing our call to lead. Our calling might take us into the classroom or the homeless shelter or our kitchens or our church offices. But it will not be limited by a job, because our calling becomes part of us, part of our spiritual DNA. The path to our calling isn't about "just" finding anything—it's about taking one obedient step at a time.

NICOLE UNICE is a Bible teacher and author of several books, including her latest, *Brave Enough: Getting Past our Fears, Flaws and Failures to Live Bold and Free*. She serves as one of the pastors at Hope Church in Richmond, Virginia.

Reflect

What is it that you can't not do?

A Big Huge Mess

Genesis 6:9–22

No way could I have done what Noah did. Building that boat with little help and for the purpose of a flood no one else saw coming. No way. But Noah did it. Faithfully. He built the ark just as instructed, gathered his wife, sons, daughters-in-law, and all of the animals and locked them in a boat just as the first raindrops began to fall.

I bet it was an utter mess. Literally. I can imagine them fighting about whose turn it was to clean up after the elephants and who was going to risk life and limb to feed the lions. They were probably constantly at each other's throats from being too long in such a small space. When I think of those people cooped up together like that, I remember when I, as a teenager, had to share a room with my older teenage cousin. We almost didn't make it to adulthood.

This text reminds me of how following God's instructions can lead you into a giant mess:

You arrive at church the first day as pastor to find that the mortgage hasn't been paid in months.

Or the musician has never been to a worship service on time.

Or the head trustee is Satan's cousin.

Or the youth minister is far too chummy with the teenage girls.

And you are standing in the middle of the sanctuary wanting to scream at the top of your lungs, thinking, *Surely I heard God wrong. Surely God could not be so unreasonable as to call me into such a mess.*

Somewhere along the way, I assumed that ministry was supposed to be neat and pleasant and rewarding. I believed that if I worked hard enough, if I did enough strategic planning, if I read enough "how to grow a church" books, then the attendance would grow, the finances would multiply, the worship would be pure and life-giving, the sun would shine. But church is messy. It's composed of people, and people are messy.

That's normal. That's ministry.

The biblical model of ministry suggests that God can and often does call us, like Noah, into situations that aren't pretty or pleasant or easy. There is something deeply liberating about knowing that. It means we don't have to take it so personally when it feels like we are running a circus instead of a church. We can put on our gloves and dig elbow-deep into the muck of our congregations and communities.

Eventually the storm will end and the waters will subside. God calls us to be like Noah, not to be the best, or the most glamorous, or the shiniest. God just calls us to be faithful, to go where he leads us—even into an utter mess.

TIFFANY THOMAS is a native of Columbus, Ohio. She earned her BA from Spelman College in Atlanta, Georgia, and pursued her MDiv from Duke University.

Reflect
What feels messy about your calling right now?

Weekend Ideas

1. Read *The Call: Finding and Fulfilling the Central Purpose of Your Life* by Os Guinness. What did you learn about calling? How can you use this knowledge to further live out your calling or help other women struggling to identify their calling?

2. Journal about how you discovered your calling. When did you know God was calling you? How did you learn the specifics of your calling? How long did it take for you to trust your calling?

3. Do something that allows you to feel fully alive and within your calling. Choose to be fully present as you do this. Then journal about the experience. How did you feel? What did you learn? How often do you get to do this kind of activity?

4. Read Philippians 1:3–11 again. Journal about the ways you've been able to discern what God wants you to do. When is it easier to hear God's still, small voice? When is it more difficult?

5. Read 2 Timothy 1:6–12 again. Journal about what it looks like to "fan into flames" the calling God has placed on your life. When have you been ashamed of your calling? Why? Bring these thoughts to God in prayer.

Group Ideas

1. Share stories about when you each discovered your calling. How did you know? What did you do as a result?

2. If your group members did something that allowed them to feel fully alive this weekend, invite them to share their experience with the group. Ask: How did you feel? What did you learn?

3. Use "What You Can't Not Do" as the basis for your discussion. Read the Scripture passage together. Then discuss: What is it that you can't not do? When have you struggled with being defined by "one job, one relationship, or one season of life"? Do you feel like your calling is truly part of you—or simply a role you play sometimes?

Week 3

Then one day a man emerged from Nazareth, teaching with authority and empowered by God. He healed the sick. He loved the unlovely. He forgave the rule-breaker. He befriended sinners. Yet the religious oppressors hated him. It was clear a new covenant was desperately needed.

Now Jesus' blood would set people free. Their old identities of condemnation, sin, and shame would be gone. Jesus offered the people (and us) a new life. They were no longer slaves to sin and brokenness but beloved children of God. Freedom and forgiveness would be theirs. A fear-driven existence was replaced by a life-giving purpose to represent God as the light of the world.

The disciples couldn't possibly understand the full poignancy and the power of Jesus' words that evening. The night grew longer and darker. Thursday became Friday. His body was broken. His blood was poured out. And heaven's victory took the shape of a cross and an empty tomb. Healing and forgiveness flowed. And we are told to remember. He is not just the God of our history; he is not just the God of someone else's testimony. He's your mighty deliverer.

Through his death and resurrection, Jesus can transform your darkest night, cleanse your deepest shame, forgive your hidden sins, and restore your wearied soul. We take the bread and wine and remember that all that Jesus did is for us here and now.

Are you held captive by your past? Jesus is the truth who sets you free.

Are you broken by your sin and shame? Jesus was broken for you and can make you whole again.

Jesus has given you a new identity and calls you into life-giving purpose. So reach out—and take this cup.

JO SAXTON leads Mission Point Church in Minnesota alongside her husband. She also chairs the board of 3DMovements.

Reflect
How can Communion remind us of our new identity in Christ?

Follow to Lead

Ruth 1:8–18

At a very early age I came to understand that as a female, I was born to follow. "Men lead. Women follow." That's what I was taught. Oh, sure, I knew about Deborah, Esther, and Priscilla, but they were "exceptions."

Having the follower mentality drummed into me, however, was actually a great way to prepare me for the day I would discover that God created women to be leaders, too. The first and most important lesson in leadership is learning you were born to follow. God's creation call for his image bearers—male and female—to rule and subdue the earth couldn't be a clearer mandate for leadership. But the only way to become the leaders God desires is to become his followers.

The person who finally taught me to think of myself as a leader was a woman whose first recorded act in the Bible was to establish herself irrevocably as a follower. When instructed by her mother-in-law Naomi to return to Moab and to her gods, Ruth digs in her heels and proved immovable, binding herself to

Yahweh. This is despite the fact that she is a foreigner, a recent convert, a newcomer in Israel, widowed, and barren—meaning she has no voice, no legal rights, and no place in society. But Ruth didn't let an unpromising resumé stop her. She is gutsy, bold, and astonishingly assertive, and all because her sights were set—not on securing a top spot for herself—but on doing whatever it took to live as a true follower of God in this world. As a result, her actions bless everyone in her path and ultimately change the world—for, unbeknown to her, she is rescuing the royal line of Christ.

Deborah's heart belongs to Yahweh, and so she calls and accompanies a reluctant Barak into battle. Barak makes the Bible's Hall of Fame (Hebrews 11:32) for great men and women of faith.

Esther overcomes her fears to answer God's call on her life. She confronts her husband (a man with the power to take her life if it suits his mood) and overthrows Haman, the second most powerful man in the world, and his genocidal plots. Her ascendance to power makes King Xerxes a wiser ruler and exalts her noble cousin Mordecai to a position of great stature and world power.

In Priscilla's unbending commitment to the teachings of Jesus and Paul, she partners with her husband in setting Apollos straight in his teaching. Together they strengthen Apollos to proclaim the gospel to countless people.

I no longer believe leadership belongs exclusively to men. God calls all of his daughters to lead. But the leadership we offer to others will only be as good as our ability to follow the one who created us to lead.

So go ahead. I don't mind if you tell me I was born to follow.

CAROLYN CUSTIS JAMES thinks deeply about what it means to be a female follower of Jesus in a postmodern world. She is the author of several books, including *The Gospel of Ruth: Loving God Enough to Break the Rules*.

Reflect

How does being first and foremost a follower of Jesus make you a better leader?

Confidence in Our True Identity

Matthew 26:26-29

n her *Huffington Post* article "10 Words Every Girl Should Learn," Soraya Chemaly examines how gender-based linguistic patterns impact our culture. She writes,

> As adults, women's speech is granted less authority and credibility. … Indeed, in male-dominated problem solving groups including boards, committees and legislatures, men speak 75% more than women, with negative effects on decisions reached. That's why, as researchers summed up, "Having a seat at the table is not the same as having a voice."

This recognition of male dominant behavior has helped women across the country, myself included, by reminding us of two things: 1) This is actually a thing that happens—we're not imagining it, and 2) It's not okay.

At every church I've attended, I've had to claw my way onto a leadership team, but I truly can't count the number of times I've been asked to help with children's ministry. The message that's been relayed to me over the past 20-something years is that children's ministry is a good place for ladies and not worth most men's time. This unfortunate stigma has removed the dignity from caring for children in ministry, which is one of the most important things we as living, breathing children of God can do.

Things need to change in order to match up with the true reality of who we are in Christ. The truth is that women are royal priests—not assistants to the royal priests (1 Peter 2:9). Because of Jesus' work on the cross, we who have been "united with Christ in baptism have put on Christ, like putting on new clothes" (Galatians 3:27). We are all hidden in Christ, as we are equal heirs in God's kingdom. We can take great confidence from our calling and identity in Christ!

Consider the ways Jesus confronted the social mores that shaped interactions between men and women in his time. Jesus taught women when it was against Jewish tradition for a Rabbi to teach them (Luke 10:38–42). He spoke to women despite their "womanly impurities" (Mark 5:25–34). He even spoke frankly to foreign women, a practice seen as ritually unclean (John 4:7–24). And he expected just as much out of that foreign woman at the well as he did out of his own disciples: to have faith.

I know Jesus values women. I do. But then I find myself apologizing for speaking up. It's as if we think it's important or expected that, as women, we begin sentences with an apology whenever we share a theological viewpoint or voice a directional idea for ministry. Why do we often feel we need to prove to those we're addressing that we have any right to be speaking at all?

As we begin to take up our true identity in Christ—who he says we are as women leaders—I believe we'll begin helping the church lead the way in treating women like Jesus treats them.

ASHLEY GRACE EMMERT is a writer, editor, worship leader, and ENFP who lives in the suburbs of Chicago.

Reflect

When has your experience as a woman not reflected what Jesus' words and actions say about women?

The Problem with Being Selfless

Romans 5:6-11

entered ministry because I wanted to live for others instead of myself. I wanted to make a difference. I was a campus minister, so I was tied to a student schedule, which meant I worked pretty much from noon until late at night. Because I'm a morning person, I found this schedule extremely difficult. I can remember walking back to campus after dinner and praying, "God, please help me not to be so selfish. I do not want to do this! I just want to stay home and unwind." Somehow, I would find the courage to face that evening victoriously, but then I'd go through the same thing the next night.

After two years, I realized I was in the wrong ministry for my personality type. I was living in exhaustion because I was not acknowledging the way God made me. It finally occurred to me that he would rather use me in a way that wouldn't burn me out within a few years. The reason it took me so long to realize that, however, was because I was convinced I just needed to overcome my selfishness.

There lay the problem. I didn't yet realize I would never be able to overcome my selfishness. When would I be selfless enough? When I collapsed? When there was nothing left of me? When all the problems I knew of were met? It was impossible! The truth is that I will never be able to overcome being a selfish human being, and I will never be able to do enough for others. Once I accepted that, I could find some sanity in my life. Even though I'd been saved by grace, I refused to live by grace. I put myself under the law, as millions of Christians before me have done. Somehow, we feel we must prove that we aren't really sinners after all.

This kind of reflection helped me see I was stuck in the old system of legalism. I believed that I had to become completely selfless in order to be a good Christian. somewhere along the line it had stopped being about helping others, but about validating my worth in God's eyes. I had to prove I was the most worthy and obedient of his servants. But you know what? I'm not, and I never will be. That's the whole point of the gospel. I am not worthy, and I'm certainly not obedient if I do something different from what God is asking me to do.

Lately, I've been aware that what God wants of me is a lot less service and a lot more pondering. He wants me to slow down enough to realize what it really means that I'm a sinner saved by grace. He wants my attention so I can spend my time doing what he made me to do, not whatever I think is going to make me so valuable to him that he can't do without me. Most of all, he's showing me that he's the Savior, who especially wants to save me from myself.

JOHANNAH REARDON loves her church and ministry, but always wants to model what it means to more faithfully follow Christ. She is the author of many books, including a family devotional: *Proverbs for Kids.*

Reflect

When are you tempted to base your worth on the work you do for God?

Keeping Your Identity

Titus 3:3-7

Sometimes, when we're not operating out of our most healthy selves, a position in leadership can go to our heads. I had poured myself into a job, a people, and a community, unknowingly letting them become the very essence of my soul. Sure, Jesus lived in the depths of my insides, too, but he shared the space. So invested was I in their hearts that when I left, I felt like the rug had been pulled out from underneath me.

While I was tooting Jesus' horn left and right, I was also making myself the shiniest star out there. Ministry had become all about me. And to be honest, it wasn't all that enjoyable.

It didn't help that I was tired, that I'd left no room in my schedule for margin and rest. For a while, I blamed it on the demands of ministry. I blamed it on weeknight expectations and weekend expectations and summer expectations. I blamed it on everyone and everything else, never seeing my lack of boundaries or lack of rest as the problem.

But the truth is, I was exhausted. I was tired of fighting to be seen as equal to my brothers, when I believe Jesus has already destroyed gender barriers. And I was tired of feeling torn in a million different directions, trying to do and be all to the community I served and my family at home. I was tired of how I was clinging to lies of "not enough": the volunteers who were not enough, the time in the day that was not enough, and the money that was never enough to do all God wanted us to do and accomplish through the ministry.

Here's the thing: ministry is qualitative, not quantitative. It's not about numbers; it's about the stories and the heart. It's about how God is making his way in and through a whole bunch of messy, imperfect, beloved humans.

But sometimes, without proper boundaries and soul care, this multi-layered, overly nuanced, full-of-messy-humans job can become really unhealthy. We can feel like we've lost our identity in the midst of trying to help others find theirs.

At the end of the day, though, God loves you simply for being you—not because of your role or title. So take care of your soul, the very essence of who you are. Invest in your relationship with God, and don't lose sight of who you are, regardless of what you do. For he calls you daughter and he calls you free. And you, dear one, matter deeply.

CARA MEREDITH is a writer and speaker from the San Francisco Bay Area. She holds a master's of theology from Fuller Seminary.

Reflect

When have you felt your identity slipping into your ministry role? What is the truth about your identity and worth?

Weekend Ideas

1. Journal about what you've been taught being a woman means. How has this understanding shaped your identity for good or bad? How does what you were taught line up with what God says about your identity?

2. Regardless of tradition, most churches don't do a great job of telling the stories of women leaders in the Bible. Look up and read through the stories of a few women in the Bible. If you're looking for suggestions, read about Ruth, Deborah, Esther, or Priscilla.

3. Look back over the Scripture passages from this week and make a list of the things God says about you. Then add in others you know to be true. Afterward, reflect: How often do you think of yourself in the same way God thinks of you?

4. Pray about the ways you are tempted to base your worth on the work you do for God. When are you most tempted to do this? What can you do to defeat this temptation?

5. Read Romans 5:6–11 again. It's easy to begin to think that only those we minister to need Jesus—but we do, too. Spend time praising God for the ways he has rescued you, saved you, and shown you mercy when you didn't deserve it.

Group Ideas

1. Have each group member read the story of a different woman leader in Scripture and share about her story with the whole group. What did you learn about these women?

2. Discuss the lies you've been told about your identity as a woman. How have these lies impacted your identity, especially as a leader? What is the truth about who you are?

3. Use "Confidence in Our True Identity" as the basis for your discussion. Read the Scripture passage together. Then discuss: How did Jesus treat women in Scripture? What does this tell us about his view of us? Why is it important to understand that we are co-heirs and co-priests, not simply assistants?

Week 4

Rest

Busyness Is Not a Virtue

Mark 6:30–32

We live in a performance-based culture that measures success by how much you can cram into your life. The more you do, the more you're doing, so to speak. This mentality has, by and large, infiltrated the church, and you don't have to look beyond the church's leadership to see that. Many pastors and church leaders are overworked and burned out, and their families suffer as a result. It feels like rest is not an option.

This over-commitment, however, is the reason many pastors are more susceptible to moral failures. One study illustrates this phenomenon well. Researchers gave each participant either a two-digit number or a seven-digit number to remember. Then, each participant was sent down a hallway, individually, where they were presented with two options: a sensible cup of fruit, or a delicious (but extremely unhealthy) piece of chocolate cake. The participants had to choose which one they would accept.

The researchers found that the participants who were trying to remember the seven-digit number were twice as likely to choose the cake. Why? According to the scientist who conducted the study, Professor Baba Shiv, "Those extra numbers took up valuable space in the brain—they were a 'cognitive load'—making it that much harder to resist a decadent dessert. In other words, willpower is so weak, and the prefrontal cortex is so overtaxed, that all it takes is five extra bits of information before the brain starts to give in to temptation."

In other words, the more we have going on in our brains and in our lives, the more likely we are to make bad decisions. Or at the very least, our busyness clogs our brains in a way that makes good consistent, decision-making difficult.

These findings have urgent implications for pastors and church leaders. We must be especially mindful that our schedules leave ample time for rest and rejuvenation. Our decisions are not just for ourselves, but for our congregations. In addition, we set an example to our churches for how to schedule their own lives. When we feed into the performance-based, frenetic pace of the surrounding culture, we risk causing our flock to do the same.

Fortunately, as Christians we do not measure our schedules according to worldly standards of success. We measure them according to a God who designed us for rest and says that it is good. Does your schedule reflect this truth?

As you rest from the important work of ministry, let God rejuvenate your spirit, building you up for the ministry work that's ahead. Rest in the truth that taking a break is not an option—it's a necessity, part of who God created you to be. May you be reminded that your worth is not determined by your busyness, but by the very fact that God created you.

SHARON HODDE MILLER is a writer, speaker, pastor's wife, and mom. She earned her PhD on the subject of women and calling.

Reflect
How have you structured regular times of rest into your schedule? If you haven't yet, how might you do this?

Healthy Boundaries
Psalm 23

When I stepped into full-time ministry as a 26-year-old, I thought I had boundaries. But there I was, halfway through the second year of my internship, blaming everyone and everything around me for my busyness. I didn't have room in my schedule to rest, let alone care for myself.

Not only did I feel frustrated by an overly full calendar, but I also felt vindicated in my anger toward the ministry I worked for. It wasn't my fault my schedule was so full. It wasn't my fault I hadn't had a weekend to myself in over a month. It wasn't my fault opportunities had presented themselves to which I couldn't say no.

But the truth is that it wasn't anyone's fault but my own. It wasn't that I didn't have time; it was that I didn't have boundaries. I was afraid to say no to any of the opportunities that came my way. I lacked the fortitude to trust God to open doors in the future. I lacked the insight to trust that life and ministry would still happen, even if I didn't have my finger in every single pot.

There's something about ministry that can make it difficult to set appropriate boundaries, and we need help to realize that we've neglected to care for ourselves. A job in ministry can be the greatest honor of all, a gift to us and those we serve. But working in the church comes with its own set of difficulties because ministry isn't merely work. Ministry is a job of heart and soul and paycheck. And sometimes, all this serving and doing for the kingdom's sake can make us forget to nurture our own bodies. This is not how it's supposed to be. The whole of who you are is not made up of what you can do for the church. The whole of who you are is Christ, plain and simple.

We forget this truth because we're doing good, godly kingdom work. We forget because we feel like women in ministry have to go above and beyond. We forget because the needs are so great, so unending, and so pressing. But this is the tyranny of the urgent. It's believing that ministry can't and won't happen unless we've extended ourselves to the point of exhaustion. This leads us to forget who we are in the process. We believe that our needs are unimportant, that the things that give us life don't matter as much as the things we're doing for the church.

It doesn't have to be this way, for this isn't the way of Christ. Christ, who is yours, rested. After ministering to the multitudes, he went away to be by himself. He rejuvenated.

He recharged. He refueled so he might be able to go and do it all again on his next journey. So, I ask you, what gives you life? What, outside of ministry, informs your sense of self? There is more to you than who you are as a leader in ministry!

CARA MEREDITH is a writer and speaker from the San Francisco Bay Area, and she holds a master's of theology from Fuller Seminary.

Reflect

What are some healthy boundaries you could set for yourself this week?

The Myth of Having It All

Matthew 11:27-30

The woman who has it all always look flawless. She's an immaculate homemaker, devoted mother, stylish decorator, exciting wife, gourmet chef, thoughtful friend, and successful worker. Before you get down on yourself for not measuring up, though, realize that the woman who has it all is a mythical creature as rare as a unicorn.

Why do we buy into this fantasy and beat ourselves up for not measuring up? Is it Jesus who's calling us to do it all? Certainly not! Jesus invites us to lay down heavy loads and weary lives in exchange for his easy yoke and light burden. To do this, we need to first embrace a biblical reality: Yes, we are not enough (and we will never be enough), but Jesus is more than enough. In Christ, we are already God's beloved masterpiece, created for good works he has planned in advance for us (Ephesians 2:10). When we stop judging ourselves by the world's values, we can stop the endless striving for more.

God promises to give us all we need for all he has called us to do. In the face of our multiple roles and overscheduled lives—especially as women in ministry—we must lean into the person God made us to be. Here are three practices that help me fight against cultural expectations and embrace who I am in Christ:

1. *You do you.* I have adopted my daughter's phrase because it reminds me to focus on what God is inviting me into rather than squeezing myself into cultural expectations that feed my ego but starve my soul. So often, we overfill our schedules because we want to promote our image as women who can do it all. We wear busyness and productivity as badges of honor. Yet, contentment and peace come when we follow God's leading and timing.

2. *Good enough is good enough.* As a recovering over-achiever, I still cringe at the thought of giving less than 100 percent to something I'm working on. But for the last decade, the Holy Spirit has been working to set me free from perfectionism. When we figure out what our top priorities are, we can give 100 percent to those few areas and let the other things be "good enough." The key is figuring out what matters most and releasing the rest.

3. *Don't write in the margins.* Just as we don't write in the margins of a sheet of paper, we need to clear and protect the margins in our lives. We need bits of time every day or every week to refuel and just hang out with Jesus. When we crowd out this space with endless to-do lists, we're more likely to succumb to the world's demands and expectations.

CAROLYN TAKETA is the executive director of small groups at Calvary Community Church in Westlake Village, California.

Reflect

Which of these three practices speak to you most? Why?

The Effects of Stress

Philippians 4:4–9

Leading while feeling stagnant and sluggish are sure ways to self-destruct in ministry. Attempting to lead others while we're frustrated, uneasy, and tired will shipwreck our leadership abilities. The problem isn't just big issues in life, but also the everyday pressures that add up and consume us. This kind of pressure can slowly chisel away at us, weakening our mental strength, and filling us with feelings of depression, isolation, and procrastination—and it can all sneak up on us if we're not careful.

Sometimes we forget that we're human—not Superwoman. Stress is the product of pressure not handled properly. We often carry too many heavy loads. Even worse, we're often the ones accepting the responsibilities. Rather than say no when we're unable, rather than make time for the most important things in our lives, we continue to take on others' loads and more responsibilities. We need to hand them over to Jesus.

Effective leadership is difficult under pressure. To lead well, we must be alert spiritually, emotionally, and physically. As a leader, I've experienced being spiritually absent when my presence was required. It was difficult for me to come up with ideas, events, or even an encouraging word for myself—and that made it difficult to support the people I lead.

At times we may run into that dry spot where nothing seems to get us excited in ministry. In such times, remember that God "will never leave you nor forsake you" (Deuteronomy 31:6). Our duty as leaders is to lead others in the direction of the teachings of Jesus Christ. We must be able to handle our own issues if we are to lead others effectively.

Unless we develop a daily regimen to keep our intimate relationship with God, it may be difficult to keep our spirit nurtured while handling so many responsibilities. Acknowledge the pressure, release your emotions, reprioritize your responsibilities, and return to the peace that God wants you to experience. He supplies us with peace that we far too easily give away to this world, peace "which transcends all understanding, will guard your hearts and your minds in Christ Jesus" (Philippians 4:7). Take the time you need to unplug and connect with God. Jesus says, "Come to me, all you who are weary and burdened, and I will give you rest" (Matthew 11:28).

An important step in dealing with the pressure in our life is self-evaluation so we can discover the areas in which Christ wants us to grow. Present yourself just the way you are to the Lord. He knows exactly where you are in your life, and he knew what it would take to get you to admit it. Put your pressures before God, and ask him for wisdom in dealing with them. After all, we're told: "If you need wisdom, ask our generous God, and he will give it to you" (James 1:5).

DEIDRA FULSOM is founder and president of Sisters Yielding Righteousness Under Pressure in Memphis, Tennessee, which encourages and motivates women to live a healthy lifestyle in spite of obstacles that may stand in their way.

Reflect
What is your natural response to pressure? What might be some healthy ways for you to deal with stress?

Soul Stress

Ephesians 2:4-10

was deep in a project at work that I loved. Yet here I was lying on my bed, unable to sleep, my brain muddled with worries. I found it difficult to breathe, a tightness clamped around my chest. If I dozed, my pounding heart would jolt me awake with rapid-fire palpitations. You couldn't tell from the outside looking in, but I was exhausted. I didn't want to see anyone or do anything. I just wanted to pull down the shutters and stay in bed.

Have you ever felt that way about work?

No matter what kind of work we do—whether we're in the office delivering presentations, cooking dinner for our families, or leading ministries at church—there comes a point where we grow tired. Burned out.

I'm not talking about the kind of tired that goes away after getting days off or catching up on sleep.

I'm not talking about weariness that would disappear if we were better organized. Even if life hums along like a well-managed project, our souls can feel like something's missing. Even though we are grateful for all God's given us, there is a kind of tired that drags us down and dulls our joy: soul stress.

Soul stress happens when the work we do becomes separated from our hearts—when work becomes a to-do, compartmentalized from who we are. The antidote is to answer this question: What feeds my soul?

This is a hard question for us to answer as women who are intentional about serving God, our family, friends, and others. But by asking this question, God transformed how I work and my choice of work by taking me on a journey to explore what feeds my soul. It's easy to focus on what we achieve and accomplish for God, when in reality God cares about who we are. God didn't make things just because he could. He chose to make meaningful things that reflect who he is. Finding work that emanates from who we are reflects God's image in us, and that can go a long way in bringing us joy and rest even in busy times. But that only happens if our work isn't motivated by the fear of not being enough, guilt, or others' expectations. It's important to choose to do things that bring us joy.

Even when we find that kind of work, though, we need to learn how to pause. In the busyness of our days, God waits for us to stop: to let go of the pressure to people-please or problem-solve, and to simply be who he has created us to be.

BONNIE GRAY is author of *Finding Spiritual Whitespace: Awakening Your Soul To Rest,* and she blogs at FaithBarista.com.

Reflect

What feeds your soul? How can you incorporate soul-feeding activities into your schedule more?

Weekend Ideas

1. Carve out a few hours to do something that feeds your soul. That might mean taking a walk in the woods, cooking an elaborate meal, getting creative with a craft, or something else entirely. The only rule is that it must be something you enjoy.

2. Take a nap. Often women leaders are running so fast that even a nap feels like an unattainable luxury. But rest isn't an option—it's a necessity. Our bodies need sleep. So get yourself cozy, and let yourself drift off to sleep without any guilt.

3. Get away into nature for at least an hour. Sit quietly, observing your surroundings. As you notice the beauty of nature, a scurrying animal, or a majestic flying bird, thank God. Allow your body to rest and your breath to slow as you sit in God's creation.

4. Journal about the ways you find your worth in your work. How might you begin to overcome this lie?

5. Read Matthew 11:27–30 again. Notice especially verse 27. What does this have to do with the rest of the passage? How might spending time with the Son, getting to know him better, actually make our burden lighter?

Group Ideas

1. If your group members decided to spend time doing something to feed their souls, share what you did. What was it like? How did you feel during and after this activity?

2. If your group members journaled, share your journaling exercise with each other. What are you learning about yourself? What do you need help with?

3. Use "Busyness Is Not a Virtue" as the basis for your discussion. Read the Scripture passage together. Then discuss: Does your schedule leave ample time for rest and rejuvenation? How is your ministry impacted when you don't get enough rest? Why do you think we believe the lie that we don't need to rest?

Week 5

Self-Care

The Importance of Self-Leadership

Mark 12:28-34

n Mark 12, Jesus was being challenged with controversial questions about taxes and the resurrection. The final question posed to him was, "Which commandment is the most important of all?" (v. 28). Jesus responded with a fundamental biblical truth known as the Great Commandment: "Love the Lord your God with all your heart and with all your soul and with all your mind and with all your strength" (v. 30). Then he proceeded to give those questioning him the second greatest commandment: "Love your neighbor as yourself" (v. 31).

When Jesus asked us to love God with our heart, soul, mind, and strength, he was saying that we should love God with all of ourselves—with everything in us. When he says love your neighbor as yourself, again the implication is to love with all of who you are. And so when I consider my life as a leader, it means leading with all of who I am for the benefit of God and others. Leadership requires all of me—my heart, my soul, my mind, and my strength. To not give all of me would be to shortchange God and others of what God has given me.

We can't lead without our heart. We can't lead without our soul. We can't lead without our mind. We can't lead without our strength. We are integrated, messy, complicated humans, and when we learn that leading from all four of these dimensions is essential, we free ourselves to lead more fully.

Before we can lead others authentically from our heart, soul, mind, and strength, however, we need to understand how this framework plays out in our self-leadership. Self-leadership is the hard work behind the scenes that prepares you for great leadership. Understanding who you are, cultivating your character, committing to lifelong learning, and developing discipline provide the framework for fostering the leadership of self. This is the grand "aha" of my leadership journey: lead yourself well to lead others better.

The great irony of self-leadership is that as we grow more effective at leading ourselves, we become more selfless. Healthy self-leadership provides the perspective from which we become more otherrather than self-centered. By tackling some of the challenges that tend to derail or distract us, we become better equipped to lead from our whole heart, soul, mind, and strength.

JENNI CATRON is a writer, speaker, leadership coach, and author of *The 4 Dimensions of Extraordinary Leadership: The Power of Leading from Your Heart, Soul, Mind, and Strength.*

Reflect

What behind-the-scenes work do you need to do so you can lead fully with your heart, soul, mind, and strength?

Avoid Compassion Fatigue
Lamentations 3:19–26

Fatigued from a sleepless night of worry, I sat frozen, staring at a list of unanswered emails. I had been coming alongside a woman in my ministry, and her email subject lines had increased in intensity over the week from "Can you help?" to "I'm hurting!" Suddenly, her one word text—CRISIS—dinged on my phone, and I burst into tears.

I was leading a support and recovery ministry at the time and felt genuine compassion for the suffering and struggles of the people in my ministry. But this particular morning, my tears were salted with frustration and exhaustion as my body and soul crumpled, overwhelmed by the weight of empathy. In shame, I shut down my computer, turned off my phone, and crawled into bed.

There is a cost to caring.

This is a difficult truth to own. Like many women called to ministry, I believe God has given me a capacity for compassion and empathy. Compassion and empathy go beyond offering condolences, advice, or rescue. They're about joining a person in grief, injustice, and loss. They mean holding sorrow and carrying burdens together. How can we empathize and show compassion without succumbing to this weariness?

If I'm going to join people in their stories, I have to know my own—including my wounds. I have to know where there has been struggle and sorrow because my wounds will be triggered by the similar wounds of others. To combat this, I must have compassion and empathy for my own story and regularly receive kindness and care for my wounds from others. It's critically important to have friends who will join me in weeping over my scars and honoring where blood has been shed and the earth scorched and burned in the battle of my own life. This provides protection and provision for my heart as I step into the wounds of others.

It's also been important for me to have regular rhythms of self-care. If you're called to a ministry of compassion and empathy, you can't put off caring for your heart and body until some future weekend retreat or getaway that may or may not ever come. You need daily rituals. It's regular self-care that brings health and healing.

There is a cost to compassion and empathy. Acknowledging that does not diminish the honor and privilege it is to enter into people's heartache. But to ignore the toll that caring takes on our bodies, hearts, and minds is actually an unkindness toward ourselves and others. Intentionally receiving daily care connects us to the heart of God. He can replenish what is spent as we love and serve others.

JEN OYAMA MURPHY is a former small-group director and support and recovery ministry director. She loves working as a lay counselor and bringing care into stories of trauma and harm. She is currently working on a master's in clinical psychology.

Reflect

Who have you let into your life to help you tend to the difficult parts of your story?

Unmet Intimacy Needs

Philippians 2:3–5

A life-giving leader is someone who lives her life by focusing on the love and grace of the Lord Jesus Christ rather than living her life by the law. Focusing on the law pushes a believer toward performance. The measure of a life-giving leader is not in the quality of teaching she shares or the prophetic word that she gives or even the number of hours she prays. It is found in the fruit that is manifested in her life when she is behind closed doors. James 3:17 says, "But the wisdom from above is first pure, then peaceable, gentle, reasonable, full of mercy and good fruits, unwavering, without hypocrisy" (NASB). The spiritual fruit manifested in her personal life is often determined by her emotional health, and emotional health is determined by how well her intimacy needs have been met. God created each of us with intimacy needs. According to Dr. David Ferguson and Dr. Don McMinn of the Center for Marriage and Family Intimacy, "we each have ten intimacy needs: acceptance, affection, appreciation, approval, attention, comfort, encouragement, respect, security, and support."

When these needs are not met, soul-wounds can occur, and a prevailing sense of worthlessness may develop. Intimacy needs are often not met for the following reasons: poor parenting or the absence of a parent, insecurities resulting in a weak sense of self-identity or self-worth, a catastrophic event in a young child's life like divorce or the death of a loved one, or sexual, physical, or emotional abuse.

When affirmation is missing and intimacy needs are not met, performance becomes the basis of self-worth. Believing the lie that love is about what she does rather than who she is, a leader may crave love and acceptance from God and other Christians. Driven to lead, she seeks approval through spiritual achievement and ministry success. Meeting a need for affirmation and approval, ministry can be used by leaders as a source of identity. Soul-wounds can be healed, but it takes being honest with yourself, humility, and the willingness to change. We can begin that work by asking God to reveal to us any unmet intimacy needs we have.

If you find that you have unmet intimacy needs, it's wise to talk about it with a trusted person. This could be your pastor, an elder, a spiritual mentor, a counselor, or an accountability partner. Whoever you talk to, you'll need both verbal encouragement and prayer support. Telling someone about your unmet intimacy needs takes great self-awareness, humility, and maturity. But in the end, it will allow you to be a better leader as you lead from a place of health.

JULIA MATEER is a writer, speaker, therapist, and director of women's small groups at Bayside Community Church, a multi-campus church in Florida. Excerpts were taken from her book, *Life-Giving Leadership: A Woman's Toolbox for Leading* (ACU Press).

Reflect
Am I leading because I am being led by the Spirit, or am I leading because it fills a need to be loved and gain approval?

An Invitation to Healing

Mark 5:21–34

One of my very favorite passages in Scripture is the story of a woman who is invited by Jesus to share her untold story. You may know her as the woman with the issue of blood. In Mark 5:21, Jesus steps off a boat onto the shore and is met by a crowd of people. Jairus, a leader in the local synagogue comes through the crowd, right up to Jesus, falling at his feet. He shares about his dying daughter and begs Jesus to heal her.

Then a woman who has been suffering with constant bleeding for 12 years silently works her way through the throngs of people. She comes up behind Jesus and reaches out to touch the edge of his robe to steal some healing as Jesus and the crowd rush to Jairus' home.

This is a story of two people and their encounters with Jesus. But it also reflects two sides of myself: a wounded woman and a respected leader.

One side of me is well-developed. I've worked hard to get to a place of leadership where I am known by name, have a title, and am afforded enough regard and respect to move through the crowd. That part of me doesn't have much trouble coming face to face with Jesus and asking for help on behalf of others I care about. That part of me knows the hurts and needs of others and can use my presence and voice as a ministry leader to advocate for Jesus' compassion and care.

The other side of me, however, is like the woman: alone, outcast, and unclean. This side of me isn't known by name and is only identified by my weakness. This is the part of me that bears the agony of secret wounds and fears, feels broken and exhausted, and is losing hope. I try to fix her on my own, but the hope for a full, rich, passionate life keeps draining away. This side of me longs for healing, but is afraid and ashamed.

Everyone, including myself, responds to, values, and regards the Jairus in me. Who cares about the woman with the issue of blood?

Jesus does.

When Jesus realizes the healing power has gone out of him, he stops everything and looks for the woman. He makes space for her to come forward to be seen and heard. He blesses her act of faith in coming forward and says, "Now you're healed and whole. Live well, live blessed!" (5:34, MSG). This is the same offer Jesus makes each of us. Will you respond?

JEN OYAMA MURPHY is a former small-group director and support and recovery ministry director. She loves working as a lay counselor and bringing care into stories of trauma and harm. She is currently working on a master's in clinical psychology.

Reflect

In what ways do you see these two people in you?

The Comparison Distraction

Psalm 139:13-16

The struggle with comparison is something many women experience. A simple glance at a polished picture in our news feed can send our minds into dangerous negative thought patterns. And ministry leaders have the added temptation of comparing their ministry to others'. I came home once from a sweet service at our church, only to scan social media and see a post from a local church plant that shared how many people attended their services that day. Instead of rejoicing with them, I felt defeated.

Then I discovered the story of Hagar, who also struggled with comparison. Hagar was a slave to Sarah—the great matriarch—and had every reason to feel less than important in comparison. On one occasion when Sarah uttered harsh comments about her, Hagar ran away, but the angel of the Lord found her and said, "Go back to your mistress and submit to her" (Genesis 16:9).

What? Submit to her? The angel must've been kidding. There is no possible way a righteous and just God would send Hagar back to such an unfriendly work environment. Or would he? The angel addressed Hagar's questions with his next shocking statement: "I will increase your descendants so much that they will be too numerous to count" (Genesis 16:10).

God had a plan, but Hagar needed to be willing to do her part. Hagar knew what this meant. Day after day, she would continue to endure ridicule from her fellow slaves. Month after month, she would face conflict with her mistress. But now she had something that would keep her going. She had a promise from the Most High God—a promise of blessing and a future for her and her son. She would have to move past the hardship created by comparison with Sarah and do the job she'd been given. She returned to Sarah and Abraham and gave birth to Ishmael. Her newfound trust in the Lord equipped her with what she needed to live a life brimming with purpose.

Each one of us has a comparison story to share. Maybe you question your abilities as a wife. Maybe you doubt your skills as a teacher. Maybe you underrate yourself as a mom. Chances are these negative thoughts began with looking at someone else—someone who appeared to have it all together. Like Hagar, our change begins with internalizing the truth of Psalm 139:16. That's worth a fist in the air and a shout of victory!

When we understand God has a unique purpose prepared for us, we can follow his direction with confidence. Comparing our ministries to others' diverts us from the path God designed just for us. And the blessings of living a life free from comparison extend far beyond what we can even imagine.

KRISTINE BROWN serves alongside her husband in ministry. She is also a writer, dramatist, and the author of *Over It: Conquering Comparison to Live Out God's Plan.*

Reflect

When are you tempted to compare your ministry to others'?

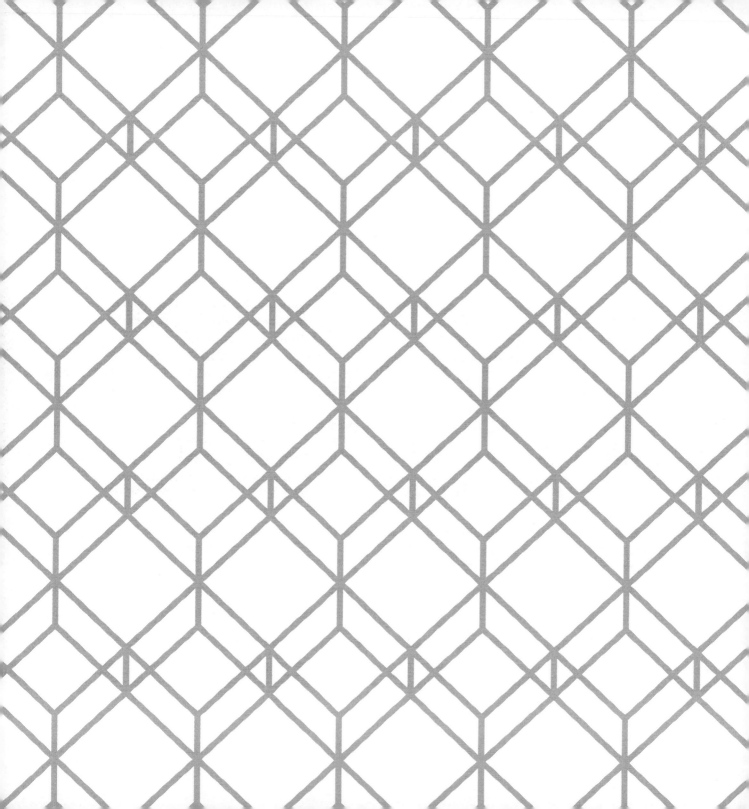

Weekend Ideas

1. Read Mark 5:21–34 again and reflect on the ways you need to be healed. Journal about this wound that needs healing and the shame and fear you feel. Then ask God to bring healing to this wound.

2. Read Mark 12:28–34 again and journal about the ways you're leading with your heart, soul, mind, and strength. How are you letting God work in each of those areas?

3. Journal about the ways you fall into the "comparison distraction." Are you tempted to compare your ministry, family, appearance, or something else? What does this temptation reveal about you? What might God be asking you to do?

4. Journal about your self-care practices. How well are you dealing with stress? Are you getting enough rest? Do you have healthy boundaries in place? Ask God to show you the areas that need some attention.

5. Spend time with a trusted friend to discuss your own self-care. Are you doing enough? What new practices do you want to incorporate? Share your commitment with your friend.

Group Ideas

1. If your group members journaled about their need for healing, share your journaling exercise with each other. What wounds have you discovered, and what steps are you taking to allow God to heal you?

2. If your group members journaled about their self-care practices, share your journaling exercise with each other. What are you learning about yourself? What do you need help with?

3. Use "Avoid Compassion Fatigue" as the basis for your discussion. Read the Scripture passage together. Then discuss: When have you felt compassion fatigue? What do you do when carrying others' burdens becomes too much? What are healthy responses we could adopt? Who knows your story—your wounds, soft spots, and tales of transformation?

Week 6

Authentic Leadership

Audacious Vulnerability

John 11:1–45

2 7 million: That's the number of times Brené Brown's TED talk, "The Power of Vulnerability," has been viewed.

That's right: 27 million—and counting.

Why has her lecture on vulnerability become a global phenomenon? Because it resonates with many of our own insecurities, fears, and deep desires. The author of *Rising Strong* and *Daring Greatly,* Brown posits that the distinguishing trait of people who have a healthy sense of self-worth is that they have "the courage to be imperfect"—they are authentic and embrace vulnerability. After 12 years of research on the topic, Brown concludes, "Vulnerability is our most accurate measurement of courage—to be vulnerable, to let ourselves be seen, to be honest."

Vulnerability—which sure looks and feels an awful lot like weakness—is in fact courage in disguise. And, outside of the TED stage, it's a form of courage we see powerfully throughout Scripture.

Martha, in grief and confusion, honestly spoke her mind to her close friend

Jesus after he'd been a no-show during Lazarus's illness and eventual death. When Jesus finally arrived, Martha offered him no greeting, instead cutting right to the chase: "Lord, if only you had been here, my brother would not have died" (v. 21). Even though she believed in Jesus (vv. 22, 27), Martha didn't hide her bewilderment under a guise of well-mannered faith.

The unnamed woman in Mark 5 bled constantly for 12 years, yet she pressed on despite her hope being dashed countless times. Physical torment wasn't her only burden; her ailment rendered her religiously "unclean." She was, in essence, an untouchable—shut out from even the life of faith, an outcast for more than a decade. Yet somehow she clung to hope. When everything in her life told her no, give up, it's over, surrender, she still believed, "If I just touch his clothes, I will be healed" (v. 28). In her desperation, she reached out to touch Jesus and was miraculously healed.

The Samaritan woman at the well dared to face her own shame—and let others see it, too (John 4). Jesus called her out on her scandalous past and present, but he also offered her grace and truth. She immediately went to tell others, and she did so by pointing right toward "everything I ever did" (v. 29). It takes courage to live in vulnerability like this—to speak with gutsy honesty, to lean into God's unconditional love.

Christian leadership takes real courage—and it's often courage in disguise. It's vulnerability and authenticity; it's the bravery to face (and not hide) our own weaknesses. "My grace is sufficient for you, for my power is made perfect in weakness," the Lord told Paul (2 Corinthians 12:9). Are you feeling desperate and vulnerable? Then you're right where you need to be.

KELLI B. TRUJILLO is an editor for *Christianity Today* and the author of several books, including *The Busy Mom's Guide to Spiritual Survival.*

Reflect

Does vulnerability come naturally to you? What positive and negative experiences have you had with being vulnerable?

The Myth of Perfection

Galatians 3:7–14

It's 100 million degrees in Chicago, and I'm sweating through my shirt. I've not showered, and I'm sporting a baseball hat and sunglasses to mask this fact, desperately hoping no one notices me. I scurry from my car into the building like an incognito A-Lister—only I'm dashing across the church parking lot to my office. It's my day off, and I'm trying to finish grocery shopping, laundry, errands, and that leadership book I left at work (again). I slide through the least visible door only to crash immediately into a parishioner, who promptly asks me the question I hate: "How do you do it all?"

I hate this question. Hate it. Does anyone ever do it all? What is "all" anyway, and who suggested that doing, having, being, and seeing it all was a good thing? This oft-repeated phrase haunts an entire generation of women. But no one does this nor should they. I serve in a pastoral role at my church, and my husband slugs it out daily as an engineer. We have three active, engaging, exhausting children. We try to make it all work, but the reality is that life is never going to work out the way our culture (or sloppy exegesis of the Proverbs

31 woman) has advertised it.

As ministry leaders, we're often expected to have it all perfected. We are, after all, leading and trying our best to represent the God of the universe who is our all in all. It's assumed that our relationships and marriages are examples of unity and balance, our families calm and organized, our spiritual journeys prayer-filled and Spirit-led. People come to us seeking these very elements for their own lives. They instinctually trust that we possess them. Tack on our cultural strivings for perfect bodies, financial success, and an endless string of friends with whom to sip coffee, and it doesn't take long to have every ounce of energy sapped from us.

What if we refused to perpetuate this life-haunting narrative? When I falsely act as though my ministry-work-life-family balance is actually balancing, I rob others of the relief and pure joy of knowing that having it all is a false construct of our culture and our own neuroses—not a spiritual goal that God has for anyone. When I share the honest tension I experience on a daily basis and my inability to succeed fully at any part of life, I remind myself and others that we stand in a long line of real people whose lives were a wreck. Just look at Scripture. Women like Ruth, Naomi, and Esther lived tense, stress-filled, and chaotic lives. The Woman at the Well was a mess. And whoa, how about David, Solomon, Moses, and Abraham? Not exactly examples of flawless, all-together lives! But for each of these people, peace and joy came from trusting God and confessing their lack rather than trumpeting their success—and we can have this, too.

TRACEY BIANCHI serves as the worship and teaching pastor at Christ Church of Oak Brook. She is the author of several books, including *True You: Moving Beyond Self-Doubt and Using Your Voice*.

Reflect

In what ways do you perpetuate the expectation of having it all together? How might you allow others to see that you don't have it all together?

Tears with an Audience

1 Samuel 1:10–20

I n theory I totally affirm that tears are normal, healthy, and helpful. So why am I so uncomfortable crying in leadership situations?

During a recent Sunday service, I broke into tears. My associate pastor's sermon spoke directly to a pain I didn't even know I'd been feeling. There was sobbing, there was snot. And I felt especially anxious because I knew that with the end of his sermon came my cue to pray, lead the offering, do announcements, and sing the doxology. I wouldn't have time to explain why the lead pastor was in floods of tears. Which is just as well, since I didn't know.

I don't use the word "hate" lightly. But I hate crying in front of people. Especially people I'm trying to lead. How can they take me seriously if they see me leaking? (Not to mention all the questions related to gender stereotypes.)

But the Bible is soaked in tears. And they're cried by all the heroes of our faith: Joseph weeps so loudly that his cries fill the whole household of Pharaoh. Jesus weeps with grief over the death of Lazarus. He weeps with longing over Jerusalem. His deepest prayers surface as tears.

Prophets weep, priests weep, kings weep, apostles weep. They cry tears of remorse, grief, longing, pain, repentance, and joy. They cry in wars, at reunions and births, marriages and deaths. They cry because they don't understand, and they cry when understanding comes. They cry when they don't see God at work, and they cry when they do.

The writers of the Bible included the tears of leaders to reveal moments of significance. When leaders were moved to repent or mourn or rejoice, it was not a private matter but an invitation for the people to join in that response. In the same way, our tears teach our people what is important, and help them to stop and sense that something significant is happening, even if we ourselves don't yet know why it's significant.

As much as it makes us uncomfortable, it's part of our call to let our people see us when we weep because of the injustice, the remorse, the joy, the frustration, the pain, the beauty. When we do, we teach them to care deeply, to be wholly present. As much as we'd like to figure that out alone and return, when composed, to dryly pronounce it, by then the moment has passed. And we have denied the community the opportunity to listen together for what God is doing.

If it's our job to let our very soggy selves reveal that something significant is happening, maybe we should get comfortable with tears. Or at least get used to being uncomfortable.

MANDY SMITH is lead pastor of University Christian Church in Cincinnati, Ohio, and the author of *The Vulnerable Pastor.*

Reflect

How often do you show emotions to the people you lead?

Find Your Voice

Ruth 2:8-12

I t's a man's world," we're told. To succeed as a leader, we must adapt our-selves to the world of men. We must learn to think and speak like a man.

While I don't want to discount the importance of understanding men and how they think and operate, we aren't men and are giving up some-thing central to who we are if we lose ourselves by imitating them. We end up distancing our very selves from the message we proclaim. We can routinely prepare and deliver messages without connecting our words to our own hearts and struggles, without tapping into the rich perspectives God has given us as women, or drawing out of our personal histories with God.

What does it mean for a woman to find her voice? Some are quick to reduce the discussion to emotions and tears. But that explanation is far too simplistic and doesn't account for the fact that a lot of men choke up when they speak about something they care deeply about.

For me personally, a better example of a woman who found her voice is Ruth the Moabitess. Ruth saw the world through the eyes of a woman, of a Gentile outsider, of a scavenger in the grain fields of Bethlehem, and above all, through the eyes of a follower of Yahweh. Her "own voice" emerges out of her richly complex perspective. She speaks from her heart, from her true self, and in using her own voice becomes a powerful agent for change in Israel.

Her words reach the ears of Boaz, a man who knows how to listen. He listens to this new voice—this female voice, this voice that speaks out of poverty, this foreign voice that dares to reinterpret Jewish law.

Boaz is a landowner who carefully observes the letter of Mosaic gleaning laws. But the gleaning practices of Israel look very different when you're living on the hungry side of the law. Ruth possesses a perspective Boaz lacks. The letter of the law says, "Let them glean." And Boaz complies. The spirit of the law (according to Ruth) says, "Feed them." Ruth's perspective opens up new possibilities Boaz hadn't considered.

What does it mean for a woman to find her own voice? I'm still pondering that question for myself. But in Ruth's case, it meant a new perspective—a missing perspective— was gained. It meant the conversation between men and women, about God and his Word and what it means to follow him in this world, grew richer and deeper. It meant Boaz, through Ruth's leadership, discovered a whole new ever-expanding realm of obedience to God. It meant God's people learned to sacrifice in greater ways for the good of those in need, and that the kingdom of God shone more brightly in the fields of Bethlehem than they would have otherwise.

Seems to me we need to work on finding our voices, too.

CAROLYN CUSTIS JAMES thinks deeply about what it means to be a female follower of Jesus in a postmodern world. She is the author of several books, including *The Gospel of Ruth: Loving God Enough to Break the Rules.*

Reflect
What unique perspective has God given you through your experiences? How are you sharing that perspective with others?

The Wounded Leader

2 Corinthians 1:3–7

'm not sure the North American church in general does the right thing on Mother's Day or Father's Day. Then again, I don't always attend church on these feel-good holidays because frankly, they don't make me feel so good. As a 40-something woman who married in her mid-30s, my biological clock ticks on, and my womb and arms remain empty. I focus on seminary, ministry, family, friends, and work, but I haven't given up hope on the fertility front. I am in that awkward in-between place, where I get asked if I want kids while women all around me suddenly seem to sprout baby bumps.

Ironically, I preached my first church sermon on the day we celebrate moms. Somehow I became the sermon-giver on the day we celebrate the amazing women who give us life. This was a turning point that could only be accomplished through the God of all comfort, who indeed comforts me in all my troubles. Through him, I am able to lead from an area of open woundedness. At some point in your leadership story—no matter what it might look like—you will, too.

My heart-wrenching questions have driven me to God's Word for answers about a woman's identity—and my brokenness has led to some transforming discoveries. Our heavenly Father does not glorify marriage and motherhood as the primary goal of every woman. These are noble pursuits, yes, but they don't define us in God's eyes. Instead, each woman is his image-bearer representative in this world; she is appointed as an *ezer*—the Hebrew word used for Eve that means warrior and rescuer (Genesis 2:18); and finally, she is set free to love God with all her heart and to obey him, no matter what her station in life. How amazing to think my empty arms give me an opportunity to encourage infertile women, singles, empty nesters, and every woman who feels sidelined somehow. Yes, even mothers! These truths make me smile despite the tears, casting my years of infertility in an entirely different light.

Second Corinthians 1:4 says we will comfort those in "any trouble" with the comfort we have already received in "all our troubles." This tells me two things about the wounded leader. First, God's comfort extends to us, no matter our struggle—grief, infertility, loneliness, health, addiction, you name it—nothing is beyond God's reach and restoration. And second, whatever your trouble is, it exists at least in part so that you can comfort others in all sorts of trouble. Understanding these truths, I can now focus on asking God exactly how he wants to use my pain as a platform that allows his comfort to overflow.

SUZANNE BURDEN is the discipleship pastor at Three Rivers Wesleyan Church and the author of *Reclaiming Eve: The Identity and Calling of Women in the Kingdom of God.*

Reflect

What woundedness in your life are you hiding that God might want to use for his glory?

Weekend Ideas

1. Watch Brené Brown's TED talk called "The Power of Vulnerability." Why do you think vulnerability is so important to Christian leadership? How might women be uniquely equipped to be vulnerable leaders?

2. Look up the stories of one or more of the women mentioned in "Audacious Vulnerability." What do their stories teach you about being vulnerable and authentic?

3. Journal about your experiences with being vulnerable, especially within the church. How has it been positive? How has it been negative? Do you tend to be vulnerable as you lead, or are you more likely to hold back your true self?

4. Women leaders often feel pressure to pretend they have it all together. Journal about this phenomenon: Is it healthy or unhealthy? Why? What would it look like to let down your guard so others could see your true self? Is it possible to be too authentic as you lead?

5. Read 2 Corinthians 1:3–7 again. Then journal: How have you been blessed by others sharing their authentic struggles and weaknesses? How are you allowing God to use your wounds for his glory?

Group Ideas

1. Share with each other your experiences with being vulnerable in the church. How have they been positive? How have they been negative? Why are we nervous to be vulnerable in the church? What is the benefit of being vulnerable leaders?

2. Share with each other how you've been blessed by others sharing their struggles, weaknesses, and wounds with you. What can you learn from these stories?

3. Use "Find Your Voice" as the basis for your discussion. Read the Scripture passage together. Then discuss: Does this description of Ruth line up with how you've traditionally read the Book of Ruth? Why or why not? How did Boaz, Naomi, and others benefit from Ruth using her unique perspective and voice? What unique perspective has God given you through your experiences? How might you share that perspective with others?

Week 7

Difficult Days

Alexander Days

Psalm 6

Are you familiar with the children's book *Alexander and the Terrible, Horrible, No Good, Very Bad Day?* When I come home and tell my husband I've had an Alexander day, he knows exactly what I mean. Some days are just like that—especially for women leaders.

Because you got the text before sunrise that Sister's family is in deeper crisis than you first imagined. Not only the crisis of faith you knew about, but now a marriage crisis, too.

Because you read in your inbox that Bob crossed over into eternity, face to face with Jesus himself, and you're sad. Even though you know he is more alive at this moment than he's ever been before.

Because today would have been Ryan's 49th birthday, but a tragedy cut off his life far too soon.

Because tragedy in a friend's life has caused an upheaval of her theology, and she wants you to help her make sense of it all.

It never makes sense. I want to stop trying to make it make sense. It never will. Why do we think we have to make it make sense? For our own sanity? For the sake of the people we love and shepherd? I believe what the world needs now is more leaders who are willing to say they don't have the answer. That takes guts, right? Humility. Honesty. Willingness to stare in the face of our own pain and doubt. It's hard to get anybody to do that, much less one wrestling under the "mantle" of leadership.

People need relationship in their pain. A wise shepherd knows when to speak, when to ask good questions, and when to allow space for silence. Sure, accurate theology has its place and time. But to a person in pain, our words (if heard at all) can be fingernails on a chalkboard. Sometimes the best thing we can do is simply sit with someone in silence.

It's a terrible, horrible, no good, very bad day. Human history has seen many and may see many more before the King comes to restore our world. But these days drive me to Jesus and his truth. I believe him, not because it makes me feel better. Not because he gives me what I want. Not because it's about me. I believe him because he's real. Because the story isn't over yet. I count the blessings so I can see them. And go to sleep believing bright hope will come tomorrow.

KELLY ARABIE is a freelance writer with experience in church ministry and pastoral counseling. She enjoys heart-level conversation and guiding people to care for their souls.

Reflect

Does encountering others' hardships drive you to find the "right words" or into Jesus' arms? Why?

A New Perspective on Failure

Galatians 6:7-10

Mother Theresa once said, "God has not called me to be successful. He called me to be faithful." I often remember this quote when I'm disappointed in ministry. We can sometimes focus on the end result rather than the One who has called us. But this is a mistake.

When I was a missionary in Ghana, I traveled with a team of missionaries to a village 16 hours away by car. The road was bumpy and unsafe. We had to hire armed guards to protect us on our journey. The final leg of our trip was to cross a dangerous river by boat—a large canoe, really—that slowly filled with water. It was midnight, and the only light we had was from our video camera. Fearful, I focused on the story of the disciples crossing the stormy lake to encourage myself while we crossed a version of our own.

Why did we take this crazy journey? We went to baptize a former voodoo priest. The ministry had presented the gospel to this man five years prior to my arrival. At that time, the voodoo priest told the pastor that he had no reason to accept Christ. He said his voodoo had served him well—he had a large family, land, health. Five years later, however, he became ill. The family said he was in a semi-comatose state, but he kept requesting that the pastor come because he wanted to accept Christ. I don't know what happened over those five years or what happened once the man fell sick, but I know that I met a man who desperately wanted to become a follower of Christ. We walked through the bushes of this remote village singing songs of Zion while this man was carried to the river to be baptized. After we dipped him in the water, he rose with sounds of joy and tears of peace.

My church in Ghana shared the gospel with this man with no immediate results, yet the church continued to push through the obstacles to evangelize in this village and many others. The church didn't lose hope, but remained faithful to the God who called them to go to places no one else was willing to go. This is a good reminder for me: we may never see the results on this side of heaven, but we are to remain faithful and endure to the end. Keep pressing forward. Don't quit. You can hear God right and still end up "failing." But if we change our perspective, we may find that we didn't fail at all.

CARMILLE AKANDE is an attorney, writer, wife, mother, and former missionary.

Reflect

Examine the times you feel you've failed at ministry. Were they truly failures, or times God was working in other ways?

When Ministry Hurts

Psalm 18:1–2, 16–19

t's true that ministry is hard. It's true that ministry takes sacrifice. But ministry shouldn't hurt.

It's the elephant in the room: women in ministry often aren't treated well. The tales of abuse are as shocking as they are numerous. Inappropriate comments about your clothing or body, members getting just a little too close or hugging just a little too long, women leaders being bullied to stay silent in meetings—these are all abuse.

Why are women in ministry facing such abuse? The answer is twofold. First of all, women get trapped in abusive ministerial environments because of bad theology. Pastoral leadership is a vocation that is steeped in the language of divine calling. We do not choose pastoral ministry—we are called by God into pastoral ministry. So even if the ministerial position causes pain, harm, or abuse, women in ministry often rationalize it by telling themselves that God must have called them to the pain, harm, or abuse. Moreover, women in ministry may normalize pain and abuse by equating it with the suffering of Christ.

They rationalize: "I'm hurting, so I must be doing something right. I must be like Christ."

And just as women with abusive boyfriends find it difficult to separate love from pain, women in ministry often find it difficult to separate calling from hurt and abuse. This is bad theology. God does not affirm or support violence, corruption, or coercion. He is the God of peace, love, and justice. If peace, love, and justice are not present in your ministerial position, then it's not of God.

The second reason women get trapped in abusive ministerial environments has to do with fear. The fear of being disliked makes many women smile and say that everything is okay when it's not. The fear of failure makes many women muscle through even the worst situations so that others won't say she wasn't cut out for ministry. The fear of dispensability makes many women endure the covert and overt messages that tell them they can be replaced at any moment with a more benign, amiable woman.

The fear of not being able to find another ministry position makes many women willing to serve regardless of negative circumstances, encouraging the mindset: "I'm just happy to be here." These fears can consume women in ministry, keeping them in abusive environments for far too long.

If you find yourself in an unhealthy ministry environment, don't quit pursuing ministry—God does not make mistakes with whom he calls into ministry. But don't endure the abuse—God does not ordain this sort of oppression. Instead, we must recreate the relationship between the church and women in ministry. Believe in your calling, hold fast to your value, and learn to advocate for yourself—and other women.

TIFFANY THOMAS is a native of Columbus, Ohio. She earned her BA from Spelman College in Atlanta, Georgia. She pursued her MDiv from Duke University.

Reflect
How have you been mistreated as a woman in ministry? How can you advocate for yourself or others who are mistreated?

Facing a Double Standard

Galatians 3:23–29

Over the last 14 years I've served in various leadership roles, from youth worker to college ministry intern to church planter to hospital chaplain to adjunct Christian college instructor to working for an urban church in Chicago. In every one of these positions, I've encountered resistance. It's not that I was banned from leadership, but that people weren't comfortable with my comfort in leadership.

Women in ministry face a blatant double standard. We are held to be equals but then chastised for expressing ourselves in traditionally masculine ways. The double standard is apparent when women are told to contribute to a discussion, but then are told they are bossy or nagging or too aggressive about their opinions. I expect more from the church. It should be a champion of equality, a refuge from the world, and a place of support and love. But often women in leadership find the opposite. They find themselves affirmed to be leaders, then critiqued for leading. Be the worship leader, but run any changes by a male leader. Take over the hospitality ministry, but don't ask men to bake. Lead a group devoted to racial reconciliation, but don't ask to have a leading voice in the church. Plant a ministry overseas, but don't be too vocal about our duty to human rights.

We women leaders are forced to find an impossible golden mean between too much and not enough. To stop this crushing pressure often means confronting our unconscious expectations about how men and women express themselves. I often wonder whether a man saying the exact same thing I had in a meeting would have received the same nonplussed reaction. All too often the answer is no because we're used to men's voices.

Every woman in ministry I've ever met, from capable church admin to small-group leader to children's ministry leader to senior pastor has experienced this double standard. We all want to be the best leader we can be in the context God has placed us in, but this pressure slowly grinds us to dust. The world already tears us down; let's not do it inside the church, too. God's kingdom is strengthened in diversity of every kind. If we want to represent the church well, we need to combat every insidious message that someone isn't qualified to serve God with her gifts. For some of us, that will mean having hard conversations with our colleagues about certain words—like bossy—and their history of silencing women. For others, it could mean mentoring and encouraging other women leaders as they find their voices. And for still others, it might mean standing with other minority voices to combat double standards of all stripes. Whatever it means for you, let's stand together as women who are called, rising above the double standard.

STEFANIE COLEMAN has a MDiv from Emmanuel Christian Seminary. She is the adult ministry director at Community Christian Church Lincoln Square in Chicago, Illinois.

Reflect

When have you experienced this double standard? What might God be asking you to do to stand against it?

When People Don't Like You

Colossians 3:11–17

When I was ordained and released to plant a church, I faced major battles. We were planting a church in a community that was largely against women in ministry, and one man actually threatened my life if I followed through with planting the church. Then, just 30 days after our first service, my husband died of a massive heart attack. Still, I had no doubt that God had called me to minister to this community.

The church plant wasn't all uphill, though. Many good things happened. The church grew with new converts, and my heart rejoiced to see people who had never been to church, who didn't own a Bible, give their lives to Jesus. Men and women, singles and couples, and children of all ages joined the church. Although the church was small, the atmosphere was vibrant. The members were growing spiritually by leaps and bounds. Within 18 months, we were able to erect a church building.

The leadership of the church and I worked hard to make sure the church was healthy. The cornerstone was prayer. Small groups were formed for everyone. Cohesion, interaction, and networking took place. The members visited each other in sickness, cried with each other in sorrow, and celebrated each other's victories. We became a family.

I was moving so fast and was so excited about what God was doing in the lives of his people that it took me a while to realize that some of the members were unhappy. When I realized they were unhappy with me, surprise, anger, hurt, doubt, and discouragement overtook me. There were only a few unhappy people, but they made their displeasure known to the entire membership. Worse, much of what they were saying about me was completely untrue. I was hit from the blind side, and I didn't know what to do.

Learning to minister to people who didn't like me—who may never like me—was difficult, but the Holy Spirit empowered me to love the hard-to-love. I learned to pray and seek God's Word first before I reacted. I also learned to evaluate complaints to see if there were any kernels of truth, and to correct any fault on my part. I discovered that hurt people hurt others, and this gave me compassion for the people who didn't like me. Finally, I learned to remember that God is the one who has called me, and I answer to him, not the people in my congregation.

It's a hard lesson to learn to love those who don't like us, but it's essential for women leaders. As we learn to depend on God, he will show us how to love them as he loves them.

DOROTHY J. HAIRE is a retired speech-language pathologist and retired founder and pastor of a non-denominational church outside St. Louis.

Reflect

Why is it so difficult to minister to people who don't like us? What might make it easier?

Weekend Ideas

1. Talk with God about your negative experiences as a leader. Invite him to stir up anything that you still need to process, forgive, or take action on. If there are any action steps needed, make a plan now to carry them out.

2. Journal about your experiences as a leader. How have your experiences affected how you lead in negative and positive ways?

3. Pray about the conflict you've experienced as a leader. Do you see any recurring themes or types of conflict? For instance, do you regularly clash with other leaders, or do you often feel the weight of others' pain? Ask God to show you any truth about yourself that these conflicts reveal.

4. Learning to minister to people who may not like you can be especially difficult for women leaders because many feel the urge to please others. Reflect on the ways you're tempted to please others to the detriment of your own health—and theirs. What is the right balance of healthy boundaries and seeking to please others?

5. Read through Psalm 18. How do you see yourself in the passage? Which parts especially stand out to you? What do you feel God speaking to you through these words?

Group Ideas

1. If your group members journaled, share your journaling exercise with each other. How do your experiences as a leader affect the way you lead in healthy and unhealthy ways?

2. If your group members reflected on your experiences with conflict, share what you're learning about yourself through the conflict you've faced. What has God revealed to you?

3. Use "Facing a Double Standard" as the basis for your discussion. Read the Scripture passage together. Then discuss: When have you experienced the double standard as a woman leader? How have you responded to it? How does the passage give you hope as you continue leading? What practical actions can we take to advocate for ourselves and other women?

Week 8

Be Bold

The Doldrums

2 Corinthians 4:6–7

'm generally energetic. Life happens and ideas flow.

I've also been depressed. And it took months of rest and medication to get out of it.

Then I've been somewhere else, somewhere that doesn't have a name, but "the doldrums" seems fitting.

The doldrums refers to a phenomenon in equatorial parts of the Atlantic and Pacific Oceans where low pressure can make the winds disappear, trapping sail-powered ships for days or weeks. There's just no wind in the sails.

My pastoral doldrums aren't bad enough to warrant time off, but they mean I'm not functioning normally. Often the doldrums looks like this: I'm just not interested in anything anymore. I don't hate my work, I just don't remember what used to get me so excited about it. Or I get emotional for no apparent reason, like the shock absorbers that help me absorb the bumps of life are shot. Or I just can't sleep. Or I find myself outside of my own life, like a critic of a movie instead of a character in it.

However the doldrums affect me, they often mean that the small choices of life and work become mechanical, as if I had to consciously control each heartbeat, each inhalation of my lungs. It's disturbing and tiring to be so conscious of things that are usually automatic.

In this low place, I'm rarely very good at the kind of Bible study that feels like I'm accomplishing something. I usually can't focus long enough to complete a full thought. So devotional time becomes a daily visualization of 2 Corinthians 4:6–7.

I lie in the dark and imagine my body entirely made of clay. Not a heavy lump of soft clay but a thin shell of brittle clay. I'm entirely empty, a fragile, person-shaped jar. As I breathe in, I'm aware that the Spirit of the living God, the God who spoke light into being, is filling this empty vessel with himself, letting every corner be touched by warmth and light. The outer shell almost wants to become thinner to make more room for him. After several deep breaths, I stand to return to my work, and I feel no less fragile in my own self. But by faith I am filled with something big and bright and beautiful enough to illuminate all creation, something that will never fade. If the doldrums make me long for the fullness of God's Spirit, they have done good work in me.

MANDY SMITH is lead pastor of University Christian Church in Cincinnati, Ohio, and the author of *The Vulnerable Pastor*.

Reflect

What does it mean to be bold in God's power? What does that look like practically?

Step Out of Fear

1 Corinthians 2:3–5

Through the years, I've talked to hundreds of women who have shared their hesitation about pursuing a ministry that they feel God has called them to do. I can't help but recognize my old self in many of them. Their arguments for not stepping into their calling may be different than the ones I had, but they're often coming from the same place as my old excuses: fear.

Is it any wonder the Bible uses the words "fear not" at least 365 times—one time for each day of the year? Fear is the enemy and destroyer of our faith. Fear changes our focus from God to ourselves; it makes us look inward instead of upward. An overabundance of fear can cause us to become self-absorbed instead of Christ-absorbed.

Even though fear can destroy our faith, we must remember a more important truth: faith has the power to expel fear (1 John 4:18). When we learn to be led by the Spirit living inside us, our fear vanishes.

God loves to use wounded, insecure warriors like us to do his kingdom work.

The Bible is filled with wonderful examples of people who felt inadequate, unqualified, insecure, and fearful when God called them. Remember when God called Moses to lead the Israelites out of Egypt? Moses made one excuse after another out of fear: What if they won't listen to me? I'm not very good with words. Lord, please! Send anyone else (Exodus 4:4, 10, 13).

I'm embarrassed to admit that I've said those same things to God. I realize now that they're all based in fear. The key to conquering our fear is first to admit that we have it and that it's affecting us. Once we've acknowledged this fear, we can pray and ask God for help. We must realize, though, that the choice between faith and fear is always ours. It may take time to cultivate the pattern of choosing faith, but over time it gets easier as we learn to put our trust in God. After all, the one who is in us is far greater than the one who is in the world (1 John 4:4).

It grieves the Spirit to see how many women have been held back and slowed down in doing kingdom work because of their fear. For women especially, there is still so little support and so much pushback. I know it held me back for far too long. Despite my insecurity and fear, though, God has continued to show up and prove that he can indeed use anyone he chooses for his kingdom work.

These days, what scares me the most is the thought of how close I came to letting fear win out and hold me back from the work God called me to. My life, and the lives of the people in our church, have been impacted in countless ways—and we almost missed out because of fear.

LINDA A. WURZBACHER is lead pastor of Blessed Hope Community Church in Rochester, New York.

Reflect

How are you allowing fear to hold you back from living your calling?

Say No to Being Polite

Galatians 5:13–18

love watching TV shows that feature a strong female lead. In the real world, though, it's more difficult to find women who speak and act in unapologetic, powerful ways. In fact, we're often taught to do the opposite. Take meetings, for example: Women are taught to be polite, while men are taught it's okay to interrupt—and there's a growing amount of research on this topic. Sheryl Sandberg has been a powerhouse in pointing out consistent gender-based discrimination in the workplace, and other women (and men) have followed in her footsteps to further explore the problem.

In reading the research, I feel simultaneously encouraged and angry. I've also been struck by the realization that this happens at church. A lot. Consider: In your small group, in a leadership position, or in opinion sharing, what do your words sound like? How do you start your sentences?

I usually start mine with "I mean, I'm not sure, but I just think that . . ."

Why is that? Why do we often feel small and powerless—rather than confident—in our communities of worship?

For me, it's because time and time again, I've seen the female voice challenged or ignored in ministry settings. For example, I know one woman who was recently told that her voice was too "high and feminine" for teaching in the church. Another female friend who is a strong leader has received consistent critiques, being seen as too bossy and harsh. Once I was called "brusque" when I took a small leadership position—and all I could think about were the men I've known who've consistently spoken more harshly and bluntly at church than I'd ever dream, and yet not a word was said to them about it.

When women take on leadership roles at church, we're frequently expected to be kind, people-oriented, and polite first and to be leaders second. The problem is that this expectation creates a cycle in which our nice, restrained way of speaking and our "no, after you, I'm so sorry" behavior earns us very little respect.

When I think about all of this, my first response is to feel angry. Angry that my voice isn't as easy to hear. Angry that my opinions are sometimes looked down upon. And angry that I might be perceived as small and bossy.

But this is not who God says we are. In fact, our identity in Christ should give us confidence to be exactly who he has called us to be. I wonder, then, how can we, as women, embody this confidence in our words and demeanor? And how can churches begin leading the way in treating women with the same respect they naturally grant men? For thousands of years, the church has been doing God's work in moving this world toward a better, holier way of thinking and doing. It's time we carry on this work as it relates to supporting women leaders.

ASHLEY GRACE EMMERT is a writer, editor, worship leader, and ENFP who lives in the suburbs of Chicago.

Reflect

When have you found yourself saying sorry, being overly kind, or not speaking up at all?

Leadership and Authority

Galatians 5:22–26

Talk of leadership, even servant leadership, focuses on the relationship between the leader and the led—which is very important. But Scripture also talks about authority: Esther defending her people, prophets standing before rulers, Moses leading the Israelites. Even Jesus, the epitome of selfless, sacrificial leadership, amazed people with his authority. Leadership may be about the relationship between the leader and the led, but authority grows from the relationship between the leader and the One she follows.

While good leaders embody both leadership and authority, parenthood taught me how to distinguish between the two. When I had my first child, I often questioned my role: What gives me the authority to shape this person's life? But now, as the mother of two teenagers, I confidently speak with authority in their lives not only because I have the title "Mother," but also because I've poured out my life for them. My voice carries weight because I'm older and wiser and because I've given so much for the sake of my kids.

My authority as a parent has informed my authority as a pastor; in both roles, authority doesn't come from my job title but from my ability to watch and follow. When I speak with confidence in decision making, it's because I have read Scripture and watched the Spirit at work in the congregation. I have poured out my heart, laid aside my rights, and invited others to pray and seek with me.

The times I've most needed to depend on the authority I receive from God are the times when I'm not accepted, when a congregant disagrees with my ideas or ministry philosophy, or when someone on the Internet argues that my ministry is not valid because of my gender. Opposition makes us want to defend our rights and stick to our guns. In these moments, selflessness is key. It's easy to think selflessness only means doing what others want, but as leaders, sometimes selflessness means doing what is good for the whole—even if it means we won't be liked. Honestly, it's easier for me to give up on my ideas than to know I haven't pleased people, but how am I serving God or others when I lead from my desire to be liked? And how is that faithful to the direction in which God is leading?

Standing strong for the sake of power and standing strong out of selfless authority may look very similar, but our hearts determine the difference. Power forces its own desires on others for the sake of the one in power. It makes the leader look strong and successful. But authority serves, listens, and speaks for the sake of others. We have won the right to speak and cast vision because of how well we have listened, how much we have invested, and how fervently we have prayed—not perfectly, but with great investment and care. We have authority because of how much we submit to the leading of the Spirit and the good of our community.

MANDY SMITH is lead pastor of University Christian Church in Cincinnati, Ohio, and author of *The Vulnerable Pastor.*

Reflect
How can you know if you're standing strong for the sake of power or out of selfless authority?

Get to Work

Romans 12:3-8

DAY 5

recently attended a conference where Jo Saxton spoke. One question that she asked still haunts my thoughts: Are you fully living your calling—or are you simply doing what you think you can get away with?

Her words made my heart pound in my chest. For far too many years, I've been afraid to fully live my calling, worried that I'd be too much for people. To be fair, I didn't come up with that on my own. I've had many people in my life tell me I'm too confident, too straightforward, too smart, too young, too honest. So I've learned to temper myself—like couching my words with "I'm not sure, but" and "This is probably a bad idea, but." And slowly, over time, I've learned to question what God tells me to do—and sometimes not act on it at all.

But God has called me to important work, and given me important gifts. For instance, God has made me particularly attuned to the tension between the way things are and the way they should be. I often feel compelled to correct and challenge the status quo. My biggest leadership challenges are deciding when, if, and how to address the gaps I see. Sometimes I get discouraged by how wide the gap is, especially in the church. This gives me two options: get angry, complain, and wallow in disgust—or actively be part of the solution.

As people who love the church and see its potential, we must choose to be part of the solution. Even when it's hard. Even when each step forward takes us three steps back. Even when it's nearly impossible to imagine real change taking root.

How do we do that? By boldly living our calling—not doing simply what we think we can get away with. Women are utterly resilient. We've had to be. After all, history hasn't always been good to us. Despite that, women throughout history have done brave, bold, audacious things in order to live their calling. And we have the honor of carrying on that tradition.

If God has called you, then who are you to say no? We can make excuses until we're blue in the face, naming all the ways the world says "no." But every "no" from the world is crushed by the one "yes" that matters: God's. The truth is, when you don't live your calling, we all miss out. We miss out on your gifts, talents, perspectives, and strengths. We miss out on seeing you serve God in your sweet spot. We miss out on being inspired by you.

So sister, do reflect on the ways the church has fallen short. Do grieve the ways we get it wrong. Then use that perspective to make a difference: to call out the things that need to change, to speak truth into the women and girls around you, and to band together with your sisters to support one another. God is working, and he has called you to join that work by boldly living your calling. So get to work!

AMY JACKSON is managing editor of WomenLeaders.com and a former small-group minister.

Reflect

What will the world miss out on if you decide to sit back and not live your calling?

Weekend Ideas

1. Journal about your experience with this devotional. What major themes is God revealing to you? If he had one action step for you as a result of this 40-day journey, what might it be?

2. Journal about the things that seem to hold you back from fully living your calling. Which can you change? Which are out of your control? What would it take to be bold in changing the things you can change? What would it take to gain peace about the things you can't?

3. Spend extended time in prayer thanking God for the person he's made you to be, the calling he's given you, and the new insights you've gained through this devotional. Pray, sing, journal, color, or otherwise connect with God, praising him.

4. Get coffee with a trusted friend and tell her what you've learned through this devotional. What new commitments do you need to make? How can your friend help you as you move forward?

5. Read 1 Corinthians 2:3–5 again. What does it look like to be bold in our weaknesses so the power of the Holy Spirit can be seen? What does it look like in your leadership?

Group Ideas

1. Discuss the things that seem to hold you back from fully living your calling. Which can you change, and which are out of your control? Then discuss ways you can support each other and encourage one another to boldly live your calling even when it feels you're being held back.

2. Give each group member a paper with her name at the top. Then ask group members to pass their papers one person to the right. Ask everyone to write an encouragement for the person whose paper they have. It can be a prayer, a word of thanks, or even something beautiful they see in the person. After a few minutes, pass the papers one person to the right and continue writing words of encouragement. Do this until everyone receives her paper back.

3. Use "Get to Work" as the basis for your discussion. Read the Scripture passage together. Then discuss: Are you fully living your calling—or simply doing what you think you can get away with? What does the world—and the church—miss out on when we sit on the sidelines? Why is it important to band together with other women?

Made in the USA
San Bernardino, CA
01 February 2017